JUDAH BENJAMIN

Judah Benjamin

Counselor to
the Confederacy

⬥┄⬥┄⬥

JAMES TRAUB

Yale

UNIVERSITY

PRESS

New Haven and London

Frontispiece: Judah Benjamin in 1845

Yale University Press books may be purchased in quantity for educational,
business, or promotional use. For information, please e-mail sales.press@yale.edu
(U.S. office) or sales@yaleup.co.uk (U.K. office).

Set in Janson Oldstyle type by Integrated Publishing Solutions.
Printed in the United States of America.

ISBN 978-0-300-22926-4 (alk. paper)
Library of Congress Control Number: 2020939635
A catalogue record for this book is available from the British Library.

This paper meets the requirements of ANSI/NISO Z39.48-1992
(Permanence of Paper).

10 9 8 7 6 5 4 3 2 1

To my loved ones—Buffy and Alex

CONTENTS

Introduction, 1

1. Charleston, 9

2. New Orleans, 24

3. Washington, 50

4. Richmond, 78

5. Flight, 128

6. London, 144

Notes, 165

Acknowledgments, 177

Index, 179

JUDAH BENJAMIN

Introduction

In 1842, Judah Benjamin, at age thirty-one already one of the most highly regarded lawyers in New Orleans and by far the most prominent Jewish member of the bar, agreed to represent an insurance firm that had refused to compensate the owners of a ship whose cargo of slaves had escaped to freedom in the British West Indies. The year before, in the celebrated *Amistad* case, John Quincy Adams had successfully argued before the Supreme Court that slaves could no longer be regarded as chattel once they had escaped to a free state. Benjamin, a budding legend among his colleagues for his breadth of knowledge and rapidity of mind, advanced a similar argument in strikingly passionate tones. "What is a slave?" Benjamin asked in his appeals brief, which would persuade the Louisiana Supreme Court to rule for his client. "He is a human being. He has feeling and passion and intellect. His heart, like the heart of the white man, swells with love, burns with jealousy, aches with sorrow, pines under restraint and discomfort, boils with revenge and ever cherishes the desire for liberty."[1] The *McCargo* case, and Benjamin's legal brief, became a new cause célèbre for abolitionists.

Yet by the time he wrote the argument, Judah Benjamin had purchased Bellechasse, a sugar plantation along a bend of the Mississippi River nine miles below New Orleans. The Jewish lawyer who had evoked Shylock's great speech in *The Merchant of Venice* owned 140 slaves, which appears to have made him the largest Jewish slave-owner in the United States by an order of magnitude. Benjamin was a man of the South; as slavery was the South's cause, so too did it become his. A decade after *McCargo*, he was elected to the U.S. Senate, where he would lend his prodigious oratorical skills to the defense of slavery against growing abolitionist sentiment in the North. And when the Civil War broke out, Jefferson Davis, president of the Confederacy, appointed Benjamin first as attorney general, then as secretary of war, and finally as secretary of state. Known as "the brains of the Confederacy," Benjamin ended up serving as Davis's one indispensable counselor.

Judah Benjamin was the most politically powerful, and arguably the most important, American Jew of the nineteenth century. He was also the most widely hated one, not only in the North but in portions of the South. Benjamin does not deserve our admiration; but like some other figures who have yoked their lives to deplorable causes, he nevertheless deserves our attention. Benjamin was an immigrant striver, like Alexander Hamilton, born like Hamilton in the West Indies and raised in poverty. And he was a Jew in a country where Jews did not occupy important public positions. Yet he shot to the highest levels of law and politics through the sheer force of his brilliance, charm, and bottomless capacity for work. Under other circumstances we would regard Benjamin as an exemplar of the great American art of assimilation; but it was to the South, and to the culture of slavery, that he assimilated.

Benjamin had the gift of being liked, or of making himself likable. A perennially cheerful man with sparkling dark eyes and a voice so beautifully modulated that few who met him failed to remark on it, Benjamin was a delightful host and an impeccable guest, an elegant figure of exquisite politesse. Yet he revealed virtually nothing of himself. Jefferson Davis's wife Varina, who knew him as well as anyone ever did and studied his character with a penetrating eye, once wrote of him, "No more reticent man ever lived where it was possible to be silent."[2] Benjamin only *seemed* to be at home everywhere. Stephen Vincent Benét, in his epic poem *John Brown's Body*, wrote of the "perpetual smile" that Secretary of State Benjamin "held before himself / Continually like a silk-ribbed fan."[3] The image captures an inner watchfulness that rarely slipped through Benjamin's air of *bonhomie;* he knew better than to disconcert his colleagues by openly acknowledging his tenuous position among them.

Did Benjamin, then, cynically orchestrate a life organized around the defense of slavery in order to ensure his rise in slave society? Quite the contrary: the cynicism, if anything, lay in his legal brief, which carried the day by pursuing an argument that Benjamin, with his native lucidity and dispassion, could very well imagine being made by an opponent of slavery, but which he himself did not share. And yet the inner recesses of Benjamin's soul remain a mystery. What did he, a Jew devoid of religious faith or even interest in Jewish history or life, mean by paraphrasing Shylock? Was he merely worming his way into the sympathies of judges bound to know their Shakespeare, if not perhaps as well as Benjamin, who could recite it by the page? Or was he also speaking to himself, or of himself, under the impersonal guise of the legal brief?

Benjamin's life remains opaque to us because he wanted it that way. In old age he told Francis Lawley, a British journalist and would-be biographer, that he "should much prefer that no 'Life,' not even a Magazine article, should ever be written about me," and further discouraged him by observing, "I have never kept a diary, or retained a copy of a letter written by me. No letters addressed to me by others will be found among my papers when I die."[4] Benjamin's published work consists of two legal textbooks and two articles he wrote about the cultivation of sugar. He succeeded very well in erasing himself from history; today this man who scaled great heights hardly registers as more than a footnote outside the very specialized world of nineteenth-century Jewish studies. What lingers, if anything does, is the bad smell of betrayal. In one of the rare references to him in popular literature, Rabbi Lionel Bengelsdorf, the fascist accomplice in Philip Roth's dystopian novel *The Plot Against America*, regales the Levins—the stand-in for Roth's own Newark family—with the particulars of Benjamin's extraordinary life. "The cause for which the South went to war was neither legal nor moral in my view," says the ponderous rabbi from Charleston, "yet I have always held Judah Benjamin in the highest regard." The exquisitely polite Bess Levin quietly gets up and leaves the dining table on a flimsy pretext.[5]

Yet we cannot be sure what, if anything, Benjamin was trying to hide. He felt nothing save pride in the role he played defending slavery and the Confederacy. He could have responded to accounts in the Northern press, which pictured him as a scheming Machiavelli, by writing his memoirs, as Davis and many other Confederate leaders did. He chose not to. Benjamin was dogged by rumors, eagerly promoted by his enemies, that he was homosexual. The evidence is circumstantial, but hardly trivial. Nothing else that we know of his life would seem to justify such self-concealment.

Benjamin's private life was not tragic, but neither was it

happy. At age twenty-two, he married Natalie St. Martin, a beautiful and willful seventeen-year-old from a fine Creole family. A decade later, Natalie moved to Paris, taking with her their infant daughter, Ninette. For the rest of his life Benjamin lived without wife or daughter, seeing them only on annual visits to Paris. Natalie brought him nothing but trouble. Nevertheless, he paid for her support without fail. He ended his life with Natalie and Ninette and her husband, in the mansion he had bought for them in Paris. He never spoke of—almost never even obliquely referred to—whatever loneliness or humiliation he felt.

Another man might have sought relief in the warm embrace of his own community. Benjamin was a Jewish trailblazer: the first, or second, Jew to go to Congress (the issue is disputed); the first to be asked to serve on the Supreme Court or to go abroad as an ambassador. (He declined both honors.) Yet those distinctions appear to have meant little to Benjamin. He did not seek out Jews. Not only did he marry out of the faith, as many of the rising class of Jews in New Orleans did, but he also refused to join the local temple. He ate pork, and attended church when it was useful to do so. Even during the Civil War, when he was subjected to a torrent of anti-Semitic abuse, he did not respond as a Jew. That said, he did not convert to Christianity, as did the other great Benjamin of his day, Disraeli. A man with his name, and his dark curls and dark skin, could hardly dismiss his Jewishness with the magic wand of conversion. Or perhaps he refused to reject a faith he did not believe in merely because it would have been useful to do so.

Benjamin had no wish to succeed as a Jew among Jews, but only as an American among Americans. Alas for him, he was no less determined to succeed as a Southerner among Southerners. In the midst of a debate over the extension of slavery, Senator Benjamin Wade of Ohio, like an antebellum Philip Roth, unforgettably captured Benjamin as one of the "Israelites with Egyptian principles."[6]

* * *

No life can be reduced to a moral tabulation—and certainly not one as strange and complex and enigmatic as Benjamin's. Yet it would be foolish to imagine a man somehow divided between his noble and ignoble impulses. It was not Benjamin's "dark side" that made him so loyal a servant of the Confederacy. The same burning ambition and far-seeing intelligence, the same mix of boldness and prudence, the same bottomless capacity for work that made him a great lawyer and an admired senator also propelled him to the forefront of the Confederate government. His life was one: he believed in the cause as firmly as he believed in the law.

Benjamin's early biographers, Pierce Butler and Robert Douthat Meade, writing in 1907 and 1943, palliated the moral crime in order to rescue the man from what they considered undue infamy. Slavery, to them, was something like a grave error. (To Butler, a South Carolinian, perhaps the error was not so very grave.) We, who recognize in slavery America's original sin and the source of cruelty and suffering continuing to this day, are inclined to regard the alleged virtues of a man like Benjamin as the mere instruments of a malevolent cause. Charm, brilliance, tact—how can they weigh in the scale against a life made possible by slavery and devoted to the defense of slavery?

Yet to treat the human attributes of a figure like Benjamin as merely incidental to the cause he served is to flatten both the man and history itself. We can learn nothing from the past if we regard history as a vast morality play whose end point is our own state of enlightenment. People commit themselves to causes that we rightly regard as terrible, whether the Crusades or the Inquisition or the imperialist conquests of the nineteenth century, for the most human of reasons—because they are blinded by vanity or ambition, or fired by religious conviction, or propelled by nothing more extraordinary than self-interest.

History is the record of great impersonal forces acting upon human nature. We are no freer of those forces, or of our own nature, than were men and women of the past; that is one reason why we profit from studying them, including those figures among them who served a dreadful master.

Nor can Judah Benjamin's own life be reduced to a moral calculus. Benjamin was richly endowed with what the ancients, if not Christians or Jews, would have regarded as virtues. He was a capacious figure. An outsider, he learned to adapt himself to each successive world to which his fate delivered him. He penetrated those worlds and succeeded by their rules. Benjamin was an epicurean in good times and a stoic in the face of misfortune. He was never known to panic, or even to lose his composure. At moments of supreme tension Benjamin's self-possession attained almost heroic dimensions. In the apocalyptic chaos of the Confederate retreat from Richmond, he recited snatches of poetry in order to entertain his colleagues and take their minds off the disaster they faced. When he abandoned them in order to save his own life, Benjamin eluded capture with the shape-shifting guile of a Ulysses.

Benjamin proved to be unsinkable, literally as well as figuratively. After surviving shipwreck and storms at sea, he reached England in the summer of 1865. Three years later he published the definitive textbook on contract law. By 1872 he had ascended to the very highest ranks of British barristers. At the splendid banquet marking his retirement from the bar in 1883, Sir Henry James, England's attorney general, observed, "The years are few since Mr. Benjamin was a stranger to us all, and in those few years he had accomplished more than most can ever hope in a lifetime to achieve."[7]

In a universe ordered by our moral imagination, Judah Benjamin's life would have ended with a terrible reckoning. But the universe is not a movie. Benjamin died in 1884 wreathed with honors, and probably quite content with the path he had hewn through life. By that time, the South had begun to cast off the yoke of Reconstruction, ensuring that the principle of white supremacy, if not slavery itself, would thrive for generations.

1

Charleston

DOUBLY AN OUTSIDER, Judah Benjamin was neither Christian nor American. His parents, Philip and Rebecca, were British. Rebecca Mendes had come from a long-established line of Portuguese Sephardim; nothing is known of Philip's background. Whatever modest advantages the young couple enjoyed derived from Rebecca's family; her older sisters had married planters in the Caribbean. In 1808 the Benjamins left London for St. Croix, a British possession, where they must have hoped to benefit from the growing Jewish population. They had a daughter, also named Rebecca, in 1809; Judah was born August 11, 1811. Their hopes for a better life must not have been realized, for two years later the Benjamins left English soil for America. In Wilmington, North Carolina, they joined a Mendes relation, Jacob Levy, who kept a store. In 1817, Jacob moved to the thriving riverside town of Fayetteville, and the Benjamins moved with him. Philip seems to have been unable to support his growing family, which would ultimately include seven children. In the spring of 1822 they moved yet again, to Charleston, South Carolina.

In the early decades of the nineteenth century the great migration of Jews from Central and Eastern Europe had not yet begun; in 1820 between three thousand and six thousand Jews lived in the United States. At the time, according to one historian, Jews were so sparsely scattered across the country, so preoccupied with eking out a living, so new to the continent, that one cannot speak of "even an unconsciously unified American Jewish community."[1] That would have to wait for the influx of the next generation. Those few thousand souls were concentrated in the cities of the Eastern Seaboard: Newport, New York, Philadelphia, Savannah, and Charleston. A few hardy souls moved westward with the pioneers, usually to serve as the town shopkeeper. Jonathan D. Sarna, a leading scholar of the American Jewish experience, describes the typical immigrant of the era in terms that perfectly describe Philip Benjamin: "lower middle class Jews stymied on the road to economic advancement."[2]

America beckoned to Europe's Jews with the same promise of opportunity it extended to all newcomers, but it also offered a freedom, both of conscience and of action, that Jews could not enjoy elsewhere. In the Europe of 1800, most Jews were treated not as citizens of their home countries but as outsiders who belonged to a dispersed "nation," and were thus governed by special laws that limited where they could live and how they could work. In America, they would be Americans. In 1825, Aaron Phillips, a German immigrant in Charleston probably not much older than Judah Benjamin, wrote to his parents to say, "How on earth is it possible to live under a government where you cannot even enjoy the simple privileges that correspond to a human being. Here we are all the same, all the religions are honored and respected and have the same rights."[3]

Of all the places to be a Jew in America, there was none

better than Charleston. Jews had been living there since 1695; as a merchant community, they were welcome in one of America's leading port cities. The Jews formed a congregation, Beth Elohim, in 1749; by 1791 the community of almost five hundred souls had grown sufficiently prosperous to raise an impressive synagogue in the heart of the city. By the time the Benjamins arrived, Charleston had the largest Jewish population of any city in the United States. Jews were thoroughly integrated into Charleston's professional life, and more prosperous on average than they were elsewhere. The city had Jewish doctors and teachers, auctioneers and shopkeepers, portrait painters, sheriffs, and even state representatives. One of the wealthiest members of the temple, Moses Levy, had moved from the Caribbean. His wife, Hannah Abendanone, is said to have been related to Philip Benjamin and to have brought him into a business partnership with Levy in St. Thomas.[4] Their son David, whom Judah may have known from Beth Elohim, would later beat him out by two years for the title of first Jewish senator (from Florida). The distinction remains contested, for by that time David Levy had begun presenting himself as an Episcopalian and had taken an old family name, Yulee, in place of the self-evidently Jewish one with which he had been born. Astonishingly, yet another Beth Elohim boy, Philip Phillips, would later move to Alabama and join Congress in 1853, the same year Judah Benjamin began his Senate tenure. The fact that three of the first Jewish national political figures grew up at the same time in Charleston testifies to the city's remarkable tolerance and sophistication.

Jews played an outsize role in Charleston's intellectual life. Isaac Harby, a playwright and literary critic, ran the intellectually high-minded *City Gazette*. Jacob Cardozo owned *The Southern Patriot* and used its pages to campaign for the daring doctrine of free-market economics. The Jews of Charleston felt profoundly grateful for the welcome they had received in the United

States. Many named their children "Thomas Jefferson" or "Madison."[5]

Most Jews, of course, did not own newspapers. They owned the shops on King Street, long the city's chief commercial thoroughfare, where Charlestonians went to buy groceries, or have clothing made. Philip and Rebecca operated a dry goods store at 165 King Street (a building that perished in a fire in 1838); the family presumably lived upstairs, in what must have been increasingly cramped quarters. An early biographer, Pierce Butler, quipped that Philip was "that *rara avis*, an unsuccessful Jew."[6] In 1827 Philip's business failed, and the family's home and shop were seized by the sheriff. The far more forceful Rebecca gained the legal status known as *femme sole*, which allowed her to take over her husband's stock without inheriting his debts. Rebecca served as the family's source of support until Judah began earning a salary in the early 1830s.

Judah was precocious from the start. Thanks to Jacob Levy, he had been able to attend the Fayetteville Academy, a prestigious institution that attracted students from across the region. Pierce Butler managed to track down a former schoolmate, R. C. Belden, who described Judah as the smartest boy in the school. "I never knew him to make an imperfect recitation," Belden recalled, "and the ease with which he mastered his studies was a marvel to everyone at the school, teachers and all."[7] Once in Charleston, Philip could no more afford to send his brilliant son to school than he had in Fayetteville. Judah may have gone to Isaac Harby's school; the records are not clear. We do know, however, that his fees were paid by Moses Lopez, head of the Hebrew Orphan Society, which helped impoverished as well as orphaned children—itself a sign of a thriving and self-confident community.

Judah had to avail himself of charity in order to go to school. He could scarcely have failed to notice his humble standing even in the Jewish social order. Nor could he have been unconscious of the striking difference in status between his parents. While Philip was humble, unworldly, and pious, Rebecca was proud, forceful, and secular enough to keep the store open on the Sabbath, to the vexation of Jewish competitors. Life at home would have been an object lesson, at least for the quick-witted Judah, in the attributes required to rise in society. He would choose his mother's path.

Judah did not have to look far to discover a world far finer than his own. The Jews of Charleston did not live even in a figurative ghetto; Judah would have had to walk no more than four blocks to the south to reach Broad Street, where South Carolina's great statesmen, including John Rutledge and Henry Laurens, had built splendid Georgian mansions. A block further west, at the corner of Broad and Meeting, stood the magnificent county courthouse, the city hall, and the somber brick mass of the Bank of South Carolina. In a society as feudal as antebellum Charleston, no Jewish boy could dream of scaling those heights; but he could fasten his mind on the refinement and pomp that money could buy. The great men of Charleston did not engage in commerce; their wealth came from the land, or from the practice of law.

The Benjamins' own neighborhood was known as Dutch Town for the large population of Palatine Germans (elsewhere known as Pennsylvania Dutch) who clustered around an immense Lutheran church a block west of King Street. It was a raffish quarter of taverns and brothels, solid brick homes and two-story wooden frame rental properties. In addition to Jews and Germans, the neighborhood included free blacks and even "hired-out" slaves, rented by their master to another employer and thus permitted to earn modest sums of money. Western Charleston petered out into a swampy inlet where children chased ducks and rowed themselves in homemade skiffs. (A marshy area in the humid South typically engendered malaria, and sometimes yellow fever, which may explain the neighborhood's working-class population.) Windmills along the coast powered saws to cut logs from upcountry into planks.

Dutch Town must have been an entertaining place for a boy to grow up—save perhaps for one baleful element. A few hundred yards away, between the Benjamin house and the inlet, lay the compound that included Charleston's workhouse, poorhouse, and jail. The workhouse meted out punishment to refractory slaves whose owners did not wish to beat them in full view of their neighbors. Slaves were beaten or whipped, at times after the bodies had been stretched on a rack-like device until their sinews cracked. Their screams would have carried well into Dutch Town.[8] If Judah had walked down Broad Street until it reached the docks on the city's eastern border, he would have passed by the Old Exchange or Custom House, home to what was then the largest slave market in the South. Since the building also served as the city's post office, virtually all Charlestonians crossed the threshold.

Black people had been ubiquitous in Judah's early life. His uncle Jacob in North Carolina had owned slaves, several of whom served the Benjamin family; Margaret, a mulatto, was the childrens' maid, while Hannibal was both a grown-up playmate and the boy's personal servant. Charleston was the only large city in America with more black residents than white. In 1822, the year the Benjamins arrived, the city had 10,653 registered whites out of a population of 24,780. Free Caribbean mulattoes, known as "browns," often attained sufficient wealth to own slaves of their own.

Slaves and free blacks did all the work in the city, whether as masons or carpenters or stevedores on the teeming docks on the city's eastern shore. Drawings of the docks from that time show well-dressed blacks promenading in their finery as well as wrestling. But the racial code was rigidly, unambiguously enforced. Even a middle-class free black had to give way in the street before any and all whites, no matter how far below him in the economic scale. The mark of racial otherness was all too literal: slaves who had been hired out had to wear a special badge identifying their status. The punishment for being caught without a badge was twenty lashes in the workhouse.[9]

Charlestonians mingled routinely with blacks; yet, out-numbered as they were, they feared their own chattels. The 1791 slave uprising in Haiti remained fresh in memory. In 1796 a group of French blacks had been accused of plotting a conspiracy; three had been banished, and two were hanged. An ordinance in 1806 forbade blacks gathering in groups of more than seven, save for funerals. A city militia in which all able-bodied whites ages eighteen to forty-five—including Jews—were obliged to serve patrolled the streets at night.

The fear, it turned out, was justified. In 1821, Denmark Vesey, one of the slaves who ran his master's business along the docks, began gathering a group of conspirators with the aim of murdering whites, putting the city to flames, and escaping to freedom in Haiti. In the home he rented on Bull Street, just north of the Jewish neighborhood, Vesey preached an Old Testament gospel, reading to his recruits from the Exodus narrative of Moses leading the Israelites to freedom. The plot was exposed on June 16, 1822, perhaps a month after the Benjamins had reached Charleston. That night, with the militia out in force, the whole town lay awake, children included. A massacre was expected at any moment. But the conspirators, including Vesey, were rounded up and subjected to perfunctory justice. The trial exposed the comforting myth that slaves meekly accepted their status; one conspirator told his master from the witness stand that his object was "to kill you, rip open your belly and throw your guts in your face."[10] Over the course of the next month, thirty-five slaves were hanged in an area beyond the city's northern border.

The Jews of Charleston read the same passages from Exodus that inspired the slave revolt; then again, so did most Christians.

Neither found in the scriptural narrative a general argument against slavery. On the only question on which Charleston's leaders divided—whether the bodies of the conspirators should be interred or handed over to surgeons for medical training, as was done with convicted murderers—Isaac Harby came down strongly for the latter in the pages of the *City Gazette*.[11] Virtually all of Charleston's Jews owned slaves; the Benjamins had owned slaves since their time in St. Croix. What's more, the city's leading Jewish merchants traded in slaves as they did in every other kind of property. Abraham Seixas, the president of Beth Elohim at the end of the previous century, sold slaves at auction. No Jewish citizen of Charleston is known to have expressed an abolitionist sentiment—at least while they remained in Charleston.

If, today, we feel shocked at Jewish complicity with slavery, we are probably thinking less of the book of Exodus than of the twentieth-century history of Jewish identification with the plight of black people, the central role that Jews played in the civil rights struggle. But that heroic role obscures a longer history. A small number of Jewish shippers and sea captains plied the trans-Atlantic slave trade in the eighteenth century. Throughout the first half of the nineteenth century Jewish merchants across the South traded in human beings. Jews went into business; slaves constituted a commodity of great value in the South; so some Jewish businessmen engaged in the slave trade.

What's more, for all the acceptance they enjoyed, Jews would have regarded their standing in society as too delicate to issue even the most modest challenge to the institution upon which that society rested. The Tidewater aristocrats of Virginia might dabble in Enlightenment theories of human equality, but only the rare citizens of Charleston—chiefly Angelina and Sarah Grimké, the abolitionist daughters of a leading family—were prepared to accept the full humanity of people of African descent. South Carolina was uncompromising on slavery; the state first threatened to secede in 1832, when the issue was the tariff, which was in turn tied to the plantation economy. A child growing up in Charleston in the 1820s would scarcely have been aware that there was another side to the slavery debate—even perhaps a young man of wide reading, as Judah Benjamin was.

Jews would not question the system on which Southern life rested, yet they had deeply absorbed the republican principles that governed the larger life of the nation. Jonathan Sarna describes a craze for constitution writing among early synagogues. In 1790, when the U.S. Constitution had just been ratified, Congregation Shearith Israel in New York (now the Spanish and Portuguese synagogue) drafted its very own bill of rights stipulating that "every free person professing the Jewish religion, and who lives according to its holy precepts, is entitled to . . . be treated in all respect as a brother, and as such a subject of every fraternal duty."[12]

The ringing American faith in individual liberty and equality was bound to clash with the old-world insistence on tradition and authority; it did so, above all, in America's largest and most deeply rooted Jewish community. In the years just before the Benjamins arrived, liberally inclined members of Beth Elohim declared their right to bury the dead in private cemeteries, thus precluding the control that temple authorities exercised over burial privileges. Religious elders struck back with a new charter in 1820 insisting that "There shall be one Congregational Burial Ground only," and, more broadly, returning "all the functions formerly exercised by the people at large" to the "general adjunta"—the temple's governing body.[13] The elders were determined to resist the tides of liberalism. Beth Elohim had imported whole the strictures of the Bevis Marks Sephardic temple in London. The adjunta laid claim to the private lives of congregants, imposing penalties for violations of the Sabbath and prohibiting members who married outside the faith from being buried in hallowed ground. Nor would they make any concession to the preferences of an American congregation: the interminable services were conducted only in Hebrew or Portuguese, languages few members spoke.

Beth Elohim's dissidents were not willing to submit to traditional authority. In 1825, forty-seven members of the community, including the Benjamins, broke away to establish the Reformed Society of Israelites. The families were younger and poorer than the typical congregant; two-thirds were native born and three-quarters were said not to be paying members of the temple. The reformers insisted on shorter services, prayers in English, and freedom to decide matters of principle on their own, in the American fashion. "They subscribe to nothing of rabbinical control or rabbinical doctrine," they wrote, very much in the manner of Protestants rebelling against the Catholic hierarchy. "They are their own teachers, drawing their knowledge from the Bible, and following the laws of Moses, and those only insofar as they can be adapted to the institutions of the Society in which they live and enjoy the blessings of liberty."[14] Judaism in America, that is, had to be an American Judaism, based on the principles of intellectual freedom and the equality of all (white) individuals.

The rebellion had begun with a request for reforms issued in late 1824 by a dozen members of the congregation—including Philip Benjamin. This was an extraordinarily bold declaration for so modest a figure. Feckless he may have been, but Philip Benjamin was also a free-thinker. Though never a leader of the rebel movement—a position occupied by Isaac Harby—Philip was chosen to play a role as a member of the Corresponding Committee, which published letters and documents from the congregation. For the next decade Charleston's Jewish community was divided between liberty and authority, new world and old. At the annual dinner of the Reformed Society of Israelites in 1827, Isaac Cardozo, a leader along with Harby, warned that the survival of Judaism in America hung in the balance. "If we do not adapt things to the existing state of human feelings," Cardozo declared, "our religion [will] suffer in the permanency of its sacred character, and future usefulness and renown." The claim was, at the very least, premature. The rebels never managed to raise enough money to build a temple, and in 1833 they returned the subscribers' funds and rejoined the temple. The spark, however, did not die, and by 1840 the traditionalists found themselves outnumbered and left to form a so-called "Orthodox" temple of their own. After further years of struggle, including in the courts, Beth Elohim became a reform temple.[15]

The breakaway movement had begun soon after Judah turned thirteen, when he would have received his bar mitzvah. We do not know whether or not that happened, because the same fire that destroyed the Benjamin home also leveled Beth Elohim and incinerated its records. It is plain, however, that Judah Benjamin inherited from his father not only the habits and the gifts of scholarship, but also a penchant for free thinking. In later years Benjamin demonstrated no interest whatsoever in religious observance, reform or otherwise; yet he remained sufficiently loyal to the faith that he never did convert.

Benjamin's intellectual talents startled his classmates in Charleston as they had in Fayetteville; it was said that the boy recited Shakespeare while shooting marbles. He had a gift for memorizing and reciting whatever he read. Moses Lopez, of the Hebrew Orphan Society, offered to pay for Judah's college education. It is unlikely that any of the Benjamins knew the first thing about American higher education. Lopez spoke of Yale, a school considered friendly to Southerners. Rebecca and Philip, eager for their brilliant son to get ahead, agreed. At age fourteen, this boy with no money and no prospects left home to attend a school located far beyond the confines of the South that catered to the children of the well-born. At this point, the fuzzy outlines of this almost freakishly smart Jewish adolescent begin to cohere into the image of the man Judah Benjamin was to become.

The Yale University of 1825 regarded itself as a bedrock of New England tradition. The curriculum and culture still bore the stamp of Timothy Dwight, the arch-Federalist and Classics scholar who had served as president until 1817. Judah Benjamin's entrance exam required him to demonstrate mastery of the works of Cicero, Virgil, and Sallust as well as the Bible in Greek and arithmetic. Ever since Charlestonian John Calhoun, the future secretary of war and champion of slavery, had graduated as valedictorian in 1804, Southerners had made Yale their preferred Northern college. Boys from Charleston constituted the fourth largest contingent, after New York, New Haven, and Hartford.

Judah Benjamin arrived on campus with a Hebrew Psalter, perhaps a graduation present from his benefactor; it is not known if he ever opened it. The first known Jew to have graduated from Yale, Moses Simons, had left sixteen year earlier; no other Jew seems to have attended until Benjamin arrived. No one was close to him in age. He was probably the least worldly, least wealthy member of his class. Yet he quickly made a place for himself in student clubs. He joined the Philocratian Society, a temperance group that required members to drink moderately and advise others to do the same, and the debating society, the Brothers in Union, where Calhoun had once shone. In 1819, a group of Southern students had broken away from Brothers in Union and another fraternity in order to form a club of their own, the Calliopean Society, whose name alluded to the classical muse of poetry. Benjamin left the Brothers in Union to join his Southern brethren. He was, in any case, a social animal. Sixty years later a former classmate recalled, "He apparently passed his time in sauntering around the college grounds or dropping in at the students' room."[16]

Judah studied the Latin and Greek authors, philosophy, mathematics, astronomy. Even as he appeared to spend much of his time chatting up his friends, as the former classmate recalled, "he easily and without dispute, took the highest standing in class, and was acknowledged to be a riddle and a prodigy of intellectual power." Judah remembered everything he read, and mastered difficult subjects at the first go. The fact that his older and vastly more sophisticated classmates didn't hate him is itself a testimony to Judah's social gifts. He seemed to understand intuitively how to ingratiate himself with his betters. The bigger, finer world he yearned to join now lay before him in the form of Yale's aristocratic student body. His rambles must have been far more purposeful than his classmates knew.

This riddle and prodigy was plainly destined for great things. Then a catastrophe occurred—Benjamin was told to leave Yale. As with so much in his life, we cannot be sure why this happened. The minute books of the Calliopean Society say that Benjamin was investigated for "ungentlemanly conduct" and that he was expelled following an investigation. Was that conduct, whatever it was, the cause of his expulsion from the college as well? Once he had returned home, in January 1828, Benjamin wrote an abject letter to President Jeremiah Day seeking readmission. "It is with shame and diffidence," he confessed, "that I now address you to solicit your forgiveness and interference with the faculty on my behalf." Benjamin insisted that his "improper conduct" reflected no wish to violate Yale's rules nor "premeditated disrespect" for himself or the faculty. He also thanked the college for its "kind indulgence to my father in respect to pecuniary affairs." Philip, of course, had never been able to pay for his son's schooling. Judah left with an outstanding debt for $64.34.

What dreadful crime did this desperate-to-please adolescent commit? In 1861, once Benjamin had joined the Confederacy, Francis Bacon, a member of the Yale class of 1831, and thus two years behind Benjamin, wrote an article in the New York *Independent* alleging that in early 1828 a series of articles, including "watches, breast pins, seals, pencil cases, penknives, etc." had gone missing. The students, he wrote, had baited a trap with thirty-five dollars, which soon vanished—and was found, along with the missing articles, in Judah Benjamin's trunk. They agreed to inform no one so long as Benjamin left the campus immediately.[17]

Benjamin prepared to respond to this grave attack on his honor with a libel suit, but concluded that he would only give his accuser free publicity. He explained to friends that he had been forced to leave Yale "in consequence of my father's reverses." Yet his own letter to President Day strongly implies that he was permitted to fall into arrears, and that the problem lay with his own conduct. It's striking that Benjamin did not, as he could have, ask former classmates to respond to the allegations with memories of their own. Bacon was a leading abolitionist and would have good reason to wish to discredit a Confederate leader; his claims can hardly be taken at face value. But Benjamin was almost certainly guilty of a serious indiscretion. In 1901, an early biographer, Francis Lawley, received a letter from the last survivor of the class of 1829 recalling that Benjamin "fell into association with a set of disorderly fellows who were addicted to card-playing and gambling," and that ensuing "difficulties" had compelled his "abrupt departure."[18]

Judah Benjamin *was* a gambler, both in the literal sense that, later in life, he was practically addicted to card games like faro, and in the figurative sense that he was always prepared to test fate, to make a risky wager of his own talents. But he was not a reckless gambler, for he knew very well how to calculate the odds of success, and to hedge against the possibility of failure. Perhaps he learned that prudence through painful experience.

*　*　*

Benjamin returned to Charleston, still a boy of sixteen. He could have banked on his considerable erudition to become a teacher and open an academy, as Isaac Harby and others had. But he might have felt too ashamed by his fall from favor to stay. Nor did Charleston offer scope for his ambitions. "Our manners are decidedly those of an aristocracy," a scion of one of the old families bluntly put it at the time. Bumptious outsiders were tolerated, but not welcomed. A Jew could ascend only inside the Jewish hierarchy. What's more, Charleston's star had begun to fade as the Benjamin family had arrived. The Panic of 1819 had depressed the prices of the city's chief exports—rice, indigo, Sea Island cotton. Why stay to witness the decline?

Benjamin had nowhere, and thus anywhere, to go. He could have gone to New York or Boston or Philadelphia, where the family of a classmate might have been able to give him a head start. Despite his disgrace, classmates still cared about him enough that they took up a collection when they learned that he had lost his pocketbook on his way home. But two years in New Haven had proved to Benjamin that he was not a Northerner. He would stay in the South. He chose, with unerring instinct, the one place in the South that would be uniquely open to a young man with nothing to recommend him save his talents and his ambition: New Orleans.

2

New Orleans

IN 1833, Charles Latrobe, a British world traveler, parked himself in front of the St. Louis Cathedral in the French Quarter of New Orleans and described precisely what he saw. First, at the horizon, the great Mississippi, "lined for upwards of two miles with ships and boats of every size as close as they can float," from "flats, arks and barges" to an armada of steamboats to "three-masters, lying in tiers of two or three deep." Then, just in front of the levée, the city's central market, piled high with "paving stones, masses of marble and granite coping stones, piles of timber and bricks, log-wood, coffee, sugar, corn, and wheat, beef, and pork . . . fruit stalls loaded with the produce of the tropics—bananas, plantains, cocoa and pecan nuts, oranges and pines . . ." The sense of wild profusion extended to the people and their crazy babble of tongues—"French, Spaniards, Americans, Creoles, Quadroons, Mulattoes, Mexicans, Negroes."[1]

Located at the spot where the Mississippi, then America's western boundary and highway, drained into the Gulf of Mexico, the gateway to the Caribbean and beyond, the New Orleans that Judah Benjamin chose as his new home was the entrepôt and boom town of the American frontier. The city belonged to the West as much as the South, and to America and the Western Hemisphere as much as either. The rise of the cotton economy after 1815, which had begun a steady transfer of population and wealth westward from the old seaboard capitals of the South like Charleston, had turned New Orleans from a backwater to a metropolis: the population shot up from 17,000 in 1810 to 46,000 in 1830. A thousand steamships arrived annually to disgorge their cargo into the ocean-going schooners that rode at anchor. The value of the city's exports was double that of Boston and triple Philadelphia; only New York shipped more goods.

Anything was possible in New Orleans, and everything was available—the worst as well as the best. "New Orleans in the licentiousness of its morals rivals the corruption of the old world," wrote British traveler Jedediah Morse in 1812. Gamblers regarded the city as a mecca, as did prostitutes, who patrolled the marketplace once night descended. Yellow fever regularly felled hundreds. Latrobe described the city as a "Wet Grave" with "mud oozing up from the pavement" and a miasmic blanket settling over the streets. The ever present chance of infection gave a nightmarish edge to the city's air of thrilling possibility. "To all men whose only desire is to be rich, and to live a short life but a merry one," visitor Henry Fearon tartly observed in *Sketches of America*, "I have no hesitation in recommending New Orleans."[2]

Yet had Latrobe turned his back to the market and the river, and looked instead into the street grid of the French Quarter, he could have described a very different New Orleans. No city in America looked and felt more like Europe. Only in

1803 had it joined the United States; over the previous century it had been traded between the Spanish and the French. The Cabildo, the old Spanish seat of government, flanked the St. Louis Cathedral to one side, and the Presbytère, marking the ancient home of the Capuchin friars, to the other. In the old Spanish streets, renamed by the French—Dumaine and Dauphine and St. Ann—one-story brick and stone houses from the first years of the eighteenth century still stood, while on the elegant boulevards—Royal and Bourbon and Chartres—the city's Creole aristocracy lived in brick townhouses that had just begun to acquire the city's distinctive decoration of delicate ironwork tracery. New Orleans was vital, as Charleston was not; but like Charleston, it had an ancient pedigree, an air of refinement, an inner world ruled by half-forgotten traditions. Judah Benjamin would find both of these sides of New Orleans congenial.

New Orleans had a smaller and less self-conscious Jewish community than Charleston; this, too, was in the city's favor from Benjamin's point of view. Scarcely more than one hundred Jews, most of German background, were living in New Orleans when Benjamin arrived; that very year they had formed their first congregation. The numbers swelled as the city's population soared over the next two decades, and Jews came to play a leading role in the commercial life of New Orleans. They served on bank boards and the Chamber of Commerce. Judah Touro, the leading member of the community and one of the city's wealthiest men, owned a fleet of ships and steamboats as well as vast tracts of choice real estate. Like almost everyone in New Orleans save the old Creole families, Jews came to shed their old identities and become whatever they wished. Hart Shiff hailed from the great German Jewish banking family that produced Jacob Schiff—but he removed the "c" from his last name to make it look more Christian. About half of New Orleans Jews married out of the faith, and then raised their children as Catholics. The hierarchy of New Orleans was too hybridized to erect obstacles to the progress of newcomers. The old Creole families married into the new wealth.

Nothing was fixed in New Orleans; neither boundaries of class nor of race. The binary black/white world of the South here blended into infinite gradations of color and status. The architect and urban designer Frederick Law Olmsted—one of New Orleans' innumerable celebrity visitors—was so startled by the elaborate racial hierarchy that he included in his *Journey to the Sea-Board Slave States* in 1855 a table of mixed-race designations, from the "Sacatra," a Spanish term denoting one-eighth white, to the French *sang-mêlé*, sixty-three sixty-fourths white.[3] Free people of color occupied a subordinate status in society, but a deeply ambiguous one. Many visitors, including Olmsted, remarked on the extraordinary beauty, elegance, and sophistication of the city's quadroon women, who occupied a kind of geisha class. Forbidden to marry, they served as concubines to members of the white upper class, a system known as *plaçage*. Gentlemen frequently entertained with their *placé* "wife" at their side. Behind closed doors, men might also consort with a "fancy," a slave girl known for her beauty, who could fetch as much as five thousand dollars in the slave markets.

Nowhere in America was the question of race more complicated than in New Orleans. On one hand, the city's mixture undermined the racial dogma that saw blacks as the degraded biblical "children of Ham," destined to servitude by the fact of birth. What was the *sang-mêlé*—one-sixty-fourth inferior? Yet for that very reason, racial boundaries had to be vigorously policed. While the term "Creole" has come down to us with the meaning "mixed," the Creoles used the term in its original meaning, as whites who had emigrated from Europe or European colonies, and would not brook any imputation of racial "taint." The law courts of the time were kept busy with suits against men and women accused of "passing" as white despite a mixed racial background.[4] The need to maintain a racial hierarchy in the face of the city's racial blend may explain why Jews enjoyed such an exalted status there: while elsewhere Jews were relegated to a lower stratum of the social order, in New Orleans their whiteness trumped their otherness. In the face of a barrier so dangerously permeable, Jews had to be recruited into white society.

New Orleans was, in short, the perfect place for the seventeen-year-old Judah Benjamin. All he wanted was the opportunity to deploy his talents to the fullest; and there he found it. He picked up odd jobs around town until he found a position with Greenbury Stringer, a notary attached to a commercial law firm. Benjamin never apprenticed for a senior attorney, as fledgling lawyers did in the era before formal legal education; he seems to have picked up the law through meticulous study and practical experience. In 1832 one of Stringer's clients, Auguste St. Martin, a Creole planter, wrote asking for an English tutor for his sixteen-year-old daughter, Natalie. Stringer suggested his brilliant young assistant. As the New Orleans aristocracy was scarcely naive in matters of sex and romance, it may have crossed St. Martin's mind that the young man would be beguiled by his beautiful and flirtatious daughter. She had already reached the age when New Orleans girls found a fiancé. In any case, he agreed.

In the ensuing months, Natalie taught French to Benjamin while he taught her English. Though a Jew, an outsider, a nobody who had been kicked out of Yale, he had the temerity to woo Natalie—or perhaps to allow himself to be wooed. Natalie was willful, spoiled, sensuous; a portrait made at the time shows a dark-eyed, dark-haired beauty with a dress exposing bare shoulders.[5] Benjamin was intellectual, disciplined, single-mindedly determined to get ahead. He had arrived in New Orleans knowing nothing about women beyond his own sisters, although we don't know how much he learned in the three years before he

entered the St. Martin household. For all her air of sophistication, Natalie may not have known much more about men than
he did about women. Had they been older, or more experienced, either might have realized how very poorly suited they
were to one another.

When Benjamin asked permission to marry Natalie, her
father suggested he convert. Despite his religious indifference,
and the city's liberal atmosphere in matters of faith, Benjamin
refused. He did, however, accept the obligation imposed by the
Church to raise his children as Catholics. That was enough.
Bertram Korn, the leading historian of the Jews of New Orleans, writes that alliances between the old Catholic aristocracy
and the rising Jewish class had become so common that the
only thing that made this one unusual was that Benjamin had
no money.[6]

At the end of 1832, Benjamin was admitted to the Louisiana
bar. In the course of making a modest living drawing up con-
tracts and the like, he embarked on a project of astonishing
ambition for a twenty-one-year-old novice: along with an established lawyer, Tom Slidell, he compiled a summary of six
thousand cases in state law titled "Digest of the Reported Cases
of the Superior Court of the Late Territory of Orleans and the
Supreme Court of the state of Louisiana." He and Slidell had
begun compiling the list for their own use, but soon other lawyers were clamoring for copies. It was donkey work, although
Benjamin had to write an intelligent summary of every case he
cited. Here was the first evidence, not of Benjamin's brilliance,
but of his capacity for punishing labor. The digest was published in 1834, and quickly became an indispensable legal aid.

Benjamin's association with Tom Slidell, appointed U.S.
attorney for the Eastern District of Louisiana in 1837, and his
brother John, a nimble political operative, brought him new
clients and new contacts in Louisiana's business world. The tremendous boom the city was then enjoying in shipping, trading,

and insurance meant that real fortunes could be made in commercial law; the intricacy and arcana of the field also suited Benjamin's gifts. He represented railroads and shipping firms and insurance companies. By 1844, working with Tom Slidell, now back in private practice, his firm appeared in thirty-five cases before the state Supreme Court and other venues.

In 1842, Benjamin, Slidell, and F. B. Conrad, with whom he also shared offices, were retained by three insurance companies in the celebrated case of the *Creole*, a slave ship whose human cargo had mutinied and sailed to the Bahamas, which as a British colony had outlawed slavery in 1833. British authorities had freed all 130 slaves, both the mutineers and the much larger group that had not taken part. One of the slave owners, Thomas McCargo, had insured his 26 slaves for $800 each against acts of piracy and "foreign influence," but the insurance companies had refused to pay, arguing that the slaves had freed themselves. McCargo won at trial, and the insurers appealed to the Louisiana Supreme Court.

Slave-mutiny cases served as early-warning signs of the coming conflict between North and South. Only the year before, former president John Quincy Adams had persuaded the Supreme Court to free slaves who had mutinied aboard the *Amistad*, a stunning decision that thrilled abolitionists and enraged the South. The logic of his client's legal position persuaded Benjamin to argue, as Adams had, that the slaves could not be seen as chattel in the eyes of the law. If, he said, the British officials on Nassau had "intervened" to emancipate the men and women who had arrived in the port as slaves, then the plaintiff would have had the right to invoke the terms of his policy. But that was not the case, because the slaves had freed themselves by reaching British territory.

"Slavery is against the law of nature," Benjamin asserted; "and although sanctioned as a local or municipal institution, of binding force within the limits of the nation that chooses to establish it, and on the vessels of such nations on the high seas, but as having no force or binding effect beyond the jurisdiction of such nation." This was a reference, as the court would have understood very well, to the *Somerset* case from 1772, in which Lord Mansfield, England's chief justice, had concluded that a Virginia slave who had reached England must be considered free, because slavery was so intrinsically monstrous an institution that "it is incapable of being introduced on any reasons, moral or political, but only by positive law." England had no positive law permitting slavery.[7] Benjamin then went on to make his striking, if only implicit analogy, between the situation of an enslaved African and Shylock's plea for the humanity of the Jews.

The argument succeeded: the judge ruled that "the insurrection of the slaves was the cause of breaking up the voyage," and thus overturned the lower court decision. But did Benjamin believe what he said about slavery? Adams had spoken passionately, and vehemently, and had refused to accept a fee for his work. Benjamin, in contrast, had already purchased a plantation. As an advocate, he had thrown whatever he could think of at the wall, including the far-fetched claim that McCargo had failed in his duty to provide a "seaworthy" vessel by shipping so many slaves, in such execrable conditions, with so few armed mates. Then he had walked away with his usual hefty fee. He would never repeat the claim that slavery was "against the law of nature," or even that it was pernicious. Had Benjamin been retained by McCargo rather than the Merchants Insurance Company, he would certainly have described the slaves as chattel.

Yet a true ideologue of slavery would not have cited *Somerset*, or perhaps Shylock. By this time Benjamin had spent fifteen years in New Orleans' mixed-race milieu. He had dined with men who kept non-white mistresses; he had seen free people of color every day performing many of the same tasks that white

people did, and demonstrating the same attributes and apti-
tudes. How could he not acknowledge the humanity of black
people? This dilemma was hardly unique to Benjamin: an entire class of slaveholders who regarded themselves as "benevolent," including Thomas Jefferson, acknowledged the humanity of their chattel even while keeping them in bondage. It was
something one had to simultaneously know and not know.

Benjamin was far too dispassionate a man to blind himself
to what he saw around him in the name of his own interests.
He knew what it was best not to know; he would not jeopardize
the position he had attained by expressing even the smallest
doubts about slavery's merits. Never outside of a courtroom
would he assert that slavery violated the law of nature. In subsequent years he would become one of the most eloquent de-
fenders of the slave system; yet only rarely would he insist on
the sub-human nature of black people that served as the moral
justification of slavery.

Benjamin had by this time established himself as one of the
bright lights of Louisiana. A daguerreotype from 1845, when
he was thirty-four, shows a slender, bearded young man with a
narrow face who gazes guardedly at the viewer. Although he
later became portly, Benjamin's face remained unlined into his
fifties. Those sparkling eyes, the jesting manner, the vivacity that
animated his whole being made Benjamin seem youthful until
he was quite middle-aged. He was thought of as "boyish"—and
sometimes, by those who wanted to take him down a peg, as
"girlish."

In 1847 a prominent local judge, J. S. Whitaker, published
a volume of encomia on the leading members of the state's bar
and bench. Whitaker's sketch of Benjamin testifies to the powerful impression the young lawyer had made on his colleagues:

> Benjamin is emphatically the *Commercial* Lawyer of our city,
> and one of the most successful advocates at our bar. . . . He

is remarkable for the vivacity of his features, his sparkling and intelligent eyes, the perfect neatness and elegance of his costume, and the finished courtesy of his manners. . . . As a speaker he is calm, collected, forcible, though sometimes a little rapid in his elocution. His voice has a silvery, mellifluous sweetness, and seldom jars upon the ear, by degenerating into shrill or harsh tones. . . . He never goes in search of flowers or metaphors, and yet when occasion offers, uses them with skill and appositeness.[8]

That voice, limpid and refined, supple and soft, riveted the attention of all who heard it. "It seemed a silver thread woven amidst the warp and woof of sounds that filled the drawing room," wrote Varina Davis of her first meeting with Benjamin; "it was low, full and soft, yet the timbre of it penetrated every ear like a silver trumpet." Over and again people would describe Benjamin's voice as a rich and elegant instrument—a flute. To a lawyer in a courtroom, or a statesman at the rostrum, that voice was an invaluable instrument. Even people who disagreed with Benjamin loved to listen to him. Yet the dulcet voice also served to disguise Benjamin's merciless attack. As Davis later observed, "Mr. Benjamin's courtesy in argument was like the salute of the duelist to his antagonist whom he intends to kill if possible. He was master of the art of inductive reasoning, and when he smilingly established his point he dealt the coup de grace with a fierce joy which his antagonist fully appreciated and resented."[9]

Judge Whitaker noted that Benjamin was Jewish "by birth," yet wondered "how far he still adheres to the religion of his father." The answer was, as Whitaker surmised, not at all. Benjamin was unobservant even by the standards of a remarkably lax Jewish community. The only Jew more widely celebrated in New Orleans than he, Judah Touro, gave lavishly to Jewish institutions and paid for the establishment of Nefuzoth Yehudah, a synagogue for the Sephardic community which came to be known as the Touro Synagogue. Benjamin did not subscribe funds for the new temple, did not attend, and did not seek out Jewish society; he did not measure himself by the standards of Jewish success. For all his erudition, Benjamin apparently knew little of Jewish law and scripture. In his memoirs, Rabbi Isaac Mayer Wise of Cincinnati, a leading figure in the Jewish community, recalled a conversation he had witnessed between the Louisiana senator and Daniel Webster, the great Massachusetts orator. The men spoke of religion. Benjamin, he observed, "had a confused notion of orthodox Portuguese Judaism"— that is, his own Sephardic tradition. "I felt very sorry that Benjamin could not cite one Jewish source," Wise wrote, while "Webster was thoroughly versed in the Bible, and had a full knowledge of history."[10]

Judah Benjamin was observably a Southerner. His manner was languid. When visitors came to his office he would push his papers aside and settle in for a long, gossip-filled chat as if he had all the time in the world. One would have pegged him not only as a man of the South but very much as a product of New Orleans' Creole culture, for he was a Francophile who loved fine food and wine (though he partook moderately, as the Philocratians had advised). Even his alleged girlishness would scarcely have seemed out of place in a culture other Americans regarded as effeminate. Yet Benjamin was also something else— the immigrant, the outsider, who works twice as hard as the comfortably ensconced native. When he had finished charming the visitor, Benjamin would turn back to his work and stay there, barely pausing to eat, until late at night. Benjamin needed tremendous reserves of discipline in order to perpetuate the gentlemanly image of leisure.

When the British journalist William Howard Russell visited New Orleans in 1861, he was struck by the high place occupied by Jews. "The subtlety and keenness of the Caucasian intellect," Russell suggested, "give men a high place among people who admire ability and dexterity, and are at the same time reckless of means and averse to labour."[11]

For the first decade or so of their married life, Judah and Natalie lived either with or next door to her parents, first on Chartres Street and then in an elegant Greek Revival brick townhouse on Bourbon Street, in the Vieux Carré, as the French Quarter was known. After twenty years of rapid growth, New Orleans was no longer the densely packed French city it had been in the first decades of the nineteenth century. Newcomers from elsewhere in the country—"Americans," as the Anglophones were called—had begun moving to the Faubourg Ste. Marie, an elegant and spacious neighborhood beyond Canal Street, the western border of the Carré. In the late 1830s, wealthy newcomers started to buy plots to build large, gracious homes in the Garden District, yet farther to the west. There one could live, not as a would-be Parisian in an old, clamorous neighborhood, but as a proper householder with a fine plot of land.

Benjamin chose to stay with his French family in their French setting. From here he could walk a few blocks to his law office on Camp Street, just beyond Canal, at the western edge of the Quarter; the most majestic bank buildings in the city, where Benjamin had important clients, stood just a block away, at the corner of Royal and Conti. The neighborhood was dense with cafés and eating houses.

Benjamin and his wife lived an eminently civilized life; but they lived under her parents' wing. When Benjamin finally felt that he could afford to live as he wished, he spurned both the warren of the Vieux Carré and the manicured plots of the Garden District for the very oldest and most refined Southern setting— the plantation. In the early 1840s Benjamin purchased Bellechasse and moved there with Natalie. Benjamin had stormed the gates of New Orleans society; now he could fashion the life he had dreamed of. He could hardly have found a more pointed way of saying, "I am a Southerner, not a Jew."

Slave owning did not, by itself, distinguish Benjamin from the city's other Jews: Bertram Korn reports that of the sixty-two Jews identifiable in the census of 1840, all but seven owned at least one slave, and on average they owned six to seven slaves. Plantation owners, he writes, "constituted only a tiny proportion" of Southern Jews.[12] Traditionally forbidden to own land, Jews typically congregated in cities and took up urban professions. Very few had the money to purchase a plantation; most of those with the wherewithal put their money elsewhere. Korn was able to locate only one other plantation-owning Jew in Louisiana. Benjamin ultimately came to own 140 slaves, which made him, according to Korn's records, by far the largest slave-owning Jew in America.

Why did Benjamin assume this enormous and costly obligation? Bellechasse was a business proposition; Benjamin had every intention of becoming a successful planter. But he must have been thinking about Natalie's aspirations as well as his own. The couple had remained childless, and had become surrogate parents for her brother Jules, born after their marriage. Whatever fantasies Natalie had spun for herself when she met this brilliant young man from Charleston had not been remotely satisfied as he worked his way up the legal ladder. She insisted on calling him "Philippe," a French version of his middle name, rather than his all-too-Jewish given name. Now, at last, Benjamin could supply her with the plantation romance to which the finest ladies of New Orleans aspired. At Bellechasse he threw lavish parties for the city's leading citizens. In 1843 Natalie, still only twenty-seven, finally gave birth to a daughter, Ninette. But whatever satisfaction that brought, motherhood must not have been the great aspiration of Natalie's life: in 1844, she announced that she was leaving for Paris, and taking Ninette with her.

Everything about this sequence of events is extraordinary. People did not wait to have children in the 1830s. Why had the couple remained childless for a decade? The later whispers that Benjamin was gay made much of this long interval, and suggested that Ninette was the child of another man. Perhaps they simply had trouble conceiving. Whatever the case, Natalie's decision to abandon her husband once she had finally given birth was astonishing. It is extremely unlikely that the exquisitely courtly Benjamin would have mistreated her in any way, at least in any way that a Southern woman of the time would not have expected. He continued supporting her, although he would have been under no legal obligation to do so. Natalie must have been very unhappy or very willful—extraordinarily insistent, by the standards of the day, on her right to her own happiness.

For any man, at any time, this would have been a terribly painful blow. For an antebellum Southerner, with his semi-feudal notions of male honor and female submission, humiliation would have added a sharp bite to the emotional pain. And it might have been sharper still for Benjamin, who had devoted his energy and talents to hewing a niche for himself in the solid marble of that culture. He had after all given his wife a plantation. What had she wanted that he couldn't give? Had he been cuckolded? New Orleans society must have wondered if Natalie had left to pursue pleasure she couldn't have with her husband. Benjamin must have writhed to imagine what his friends and colleagues, and perfect strangers all over town, were saying to one another.

Yet Benjamin appears never to have expressed bitterness toward Natalie. Instead he began a routine of visiting her and Ninette, and of paying for the whims of the one and the upkeep of the other, that would last almost forty years. Rumors of Natalie's affairs, which circulated in New Orleans and later in Washington, would only have deepened his sense of shame. In the louche atmosphere of New Orleans, Benjamin could have taken a mistress, or had affairs, without provoking much more than a wink from society. There is some reason to believe that even the saintly Judah Touro, a pious philanthropist of the most austere habits, kept a free woman of color and perhaps had a child by her.[13] (Touro, however, was unmarried.) By all accounts, Benjamin remained true to a marriage that his wife had abandoned. This extraordinary, one-sided fidelity fueled the rumors that he was gay. Why would he not seek the consolations to which he was entitled?

Certainly the life that Benjamin proceeded to build in Natalie's absence would have appealed to a wealthy, deeply closeted gay man. He asked his mother, his widowed older sister Rebecca, and her daughter, Leah, to come join him. They became the family of which Natalie had deprived him. Benjamin then tore down the old manor building and reared a palace in its place. Each floor of the squared-off structure had deep porches supported by massive rectangular pillars. Inside, the curving central stairway was built of mahogany; the doorknobs were covered in silver plate. Benjamin filled Bellechasse with crystal chandeliers, Italian statuary, fine silver and china plate. It was said that he had poured two hundred silver dollars into the great bell that stood before the house in order to announce visitors with the sweetest and clearest ring—the ring of the owner's own silver voice. Benjamin had the tastes and instincts of a bon vivant; with Rebecca as hostess and organizer, he threw delightful parties. He and guests played *bouts rimés*—the French pastime of writing poems to fit chosen end rhymes—and he challenged them to guess the source of literary quotations. He told ghost stories. If Benjamin felt pangs of loneliness when the guests departed, no one, save perhaps Rebecca, his confidante, knew the truth.

For all the archaic elements of plantation life that Benjamin found so endearing, his work made him more a modern capitalist than a traditional farmer. Sugar occupied a distinctive place in the plantation hierarchy. No other crop imposed such immense strains on slave workers, or inspired such fears in them, yet no other crop required such large capital investments, and offered such scope for technological improvement. Sugar cultivation required a forward-looking businessman comfortable with a practice that arose in mankind's darkest past. Sugar planters not only grew the crop but processed it on site, since the sugar in cane juice would spoil or degrade in the course of transportation. By the 1840s planters had begun to use steam-powered mills as well as drainage machines. A plantation as large as Benjamin's could cost as much as $150,000 to fully outfit, but the worldwide demand for sugar meant that a planter with the money and the patience to endure difficult years could make a fortune. Many of the leading businessmen in and around New Orleans, men who knew their way around the bank and the stock exchange, bought sugar plantations in the 1840s and '50s. By midcentury, Louisiana had more than fifteen hundred sugar plantations worked by 125,000 slaves producing one-quarter of the world's exportable sugar.[14]

Benjamin threw himself into agricultural improvement with the crusading spirit of one of Tolstoy's rural reformers. He had a gift for grasping and organizing great masses of detail, which suited him very well for his new role. In the course of his annual trips to France to visit Natalie and little Ninette, Benjamin attended scientific meetings, met with leading chemists, and read the cutting-edge journals of the day. He returned fired with new ideas and inventions that, in collaboration with a partner, Theodore Packwood, he tried out in Bellechasse. Pierce Butler, an early biographer and the product of an old Southern plantation family, writes that American sugar planting operated along primitive lines in the mid-nineteenth century: "There was no science in the process, and consequently much waste."[15] Benjamin's intelligence, Butler writes, "added to his superior advantages through foreign travel, knowledge of foreign languages, and naturally scientific habits of mind, gave him a preeminence in a business in which men who had been at it all their lives regarded him somewhat enviously and contemptuously as an unpractical theorist and a tyro."

Here, for once, Benjamin left behind a record of his thoughts and deeds. In 1848, *De Bow's Review*, a Southern journal devoted to progress in agriculture and industry, published two long articles by Benjamin, originally designed as speeches, on new methods in the cultivation of sugar. The texts are highly technical. Benjamin describes the vast discrepancy between the rough-and-ready approach of American plantation owners and the French commitment to science and technological progress. Despite the fact that the sugar beets grown in France contained far less sugar than the cane used in the South, the French were able to extract so much more pure sugar that "the loud complaints of the latter extorted a legislative enactment avowedly intended to destroy the beet-sugar industry."[16] The tariff had not worked, Benjamin reported to what must have been a rather vexed readership, for the French had responded with further technological improvements that had diminished the need for imports from the United States.

Benjamin then took his readers through every stage of the cultivation process. Americans were losing juice by operating crushing machines at too high a speed; a plantation in Martinique had demonstrated that more juice could be extracted by first "macerating" cane into thin slices. At Bellechasse he and Packwood had demonstrated that "vacuum pans" could be used to extract extremely pure crystal from sugar syrup. Benjamin explained the technique with the combination of exacting detail and bright clarity that he brought to the defense of insurance companies against dubious claims. Butler writes that while Benjamin did not pioneer the technique, he was the first to disseminate its use. He had spent $30,000 to buy the vacuum pan system from its inventor, Norbert Rillieux.

Reading this account, one imagines the exuberant Benjamin bent over drawings with Packwood and Rillieux. Yet virtually every single person around them would have been a slave. It was widely believed in Louisiana that no white man could survive the fierce heat and humidity, the flies and the disease, and the backbreaking labor of sugar cultivation. The very word "Louisiana" struck terror in the hearts of slaves elsewhere. As Jacob Stroyer, a former slave, wrote, "Louisiana was considered by the slaves a place of slaughter, so those who were going there did not expect to see their friends again."[17] In the 1840s a group of slaves on a Florida plantation staged a mass escape when they learned they were to be transported to Louisiana for sale. In his history of the Louisiana sugar plantation, Richard Follett writes, "The grueling rigors of the sugar industry placed an unfathomable strain on the human body."[18] At the New Orleans slave market, sugar planters were known to almost exclusively purchase brawny young men of eighteen to twenty-five; no one else could manage the work.

Because cane grows in swampy soil, prodigious labor was required to clear the ground for a new field: slaves felled vast trees, tore up the roots, burned the logs, plowed the flattened earth, drained the surrounding land, erected levees against the river. What's more, unlike cotton, sugar required year-round, non-stop work. Solomon Northup, the free black man who was sold into slavery and later wrote *Twelve Years a Slave*, worked on several Louisiana sugar plantations and wrote an extensive account of their operation. Between January and April, Northup explains, three teams of work gangs planted the cane (though one crop of seedlings lasted for three years). The first cut short lengths of cane reserved from the year before, the second planted the cane in prepared beds, and the third covered the cane with earth. This continued until April. For the next four months—the hottest time of the year—slaves would hoe the earth around the cane three times over, bringing fresh soil to the roots. The smallest children weeded the ground or burned felled logs; boys carried water to the field hands. Other gangs drained the soil and reinforced the levees. Slaves spent the ensuing months making repairs and cutting and carting wood, the fuel for the giant kettles.

A cane harvest, and the subsequent grinding, required a concentrated fury of work. Three slaves armed with a long, tapering cutlass formed up along the cane brakes, and as they proceeded down the row sheared off the branches, cut off the tops, severed the cane at the root and placed it beside them, where it would be scooped up by younger slaves following behind with a wheelbarrow. The imperative to cut all the cane before frost set in compelled an industrial pace; slaves who fell behind would be whipped. Others fell ill from the heat or exhaustion, or suffered injuries from the wicked blade. The mortality rate was fearsome. The moment the cane was harvested, the process of manufacture began. During this final period, which could last two months, slaves were expected to work eighteen hours a day. Slave children stood along a vast belt, feeding the cane into the rollers. Other slaves fed the fires, filled the hogsheads with refined sugar, and tended to the equipment. Indeed, one of the striking features of the sugar plantation is that slaves served as engineers and mechanics, highly skilled jobs for which they would have been well compensated as free men. By the end of the year, sugar had been dispatched to the market and the time had come for new planting.

We do not know what it was like to be a slave at Bellechasse. Pierce Butler spoke to several of Benjamin's former slaves, who testified to his relative benevolence. That may be, yet Benjamin could not have avoided the ugliest aspect of slavery: the buying and selling of humans. The mortality rates on sugar plantations necessitated a regular replenishment of human stock. Cane work also required far more men than women, sometimes in a ratio as high as seven to one; ordinary reproduction could not supply enough workers. Because slaves represented capital in human form, masters typically did their own purchasing. New Orleans was the slave-market capital of the South: tens of thousands of slaves passed through the central mart at the corner of Chartres and Esplanade, in the French Quarter. Others were sold in specialty markets in the St. Charles Hotel and elsewhere in town, including a few blocks from Benjamin's offices on Camp Street. Frederick Bancroft, an early slave historian, writes of New Orleans, "Slave-trading there had a peculiar dash: it rejoiced in its display and prosperity; it felt unashamed, almost proud."[19]

In the slave pens, Judah Benjamin would have come to know something else that perhaps he would rather not know: that children were torn from the arms of their mothers, and husbands taken from wives. And when these dreadful partings occurred, these very human people reacted with grief and rage, just as white people did. "His passions and feelings may in some respect not be as fervid and delicate as that of the white, nor his intellect as acute," Benjamin had said in the *Creole* case; "but passions and feelings he has."

By the middle of the 1840s, Judah Benjamin had rooted himself deeply in New Orleans society. In 1844, he joined the Whig party and ran for a seat in the state General Assembly. Henry Clay, the Whigs' leading, though now fading, light, had long championed what he called the "American System," a nationalist program of active government promoting industrial development and infrastructure. Slave society had turned many plantation owners against the very American faith in progress and improvement; Southerners like Benjamin who dreamed of erecting a modern capitalist economy on the foundation of a slave society joined the Whigs. While Democrats professed a Jeffersonian faith in the wisdom of the common man, Whigs worried about the broad extension of the franchise and looked to Christian society to perform the work of civilization. The Whigs were the party of urban elites. Benjamin, who had gone to such lengths to civilize himself, and had spent his life ingratiating himself with elites, was virtually the ideal type of the Southern Whig. His office soon became the party's municipal nerve center. With the support of Tom and John Slidell, fixtures in state and local politics, Benjamin was elected.

The following year, Benjamin ran to serve as one of the two representatives from New Orleans at the state convention charged with rewriting the Louisiana constitution. Once again, he succeeded. There, for the first time, Benjamin had reason to publicly air his views of slavery; no hint remained of the qualms he had expressed in the *Creole* case. Delegates from rural parts of the state proposed to adopt the provision in the U.S. Constitution that counted slaves as three-fifths of a person in apportioning congressional seats. Doing so would diminish the representation of the urbanites Benjamin represented, since proportionally they owned far fewer slaves. Rather than expose this obvious political calculus, Benjamin slyly observed that his opponents "are for giving the slaves political consequences—the very thing for which the Abolitionists have been for years contending. I am for regarding them as they are regarded by the law—mere property." If slaves deserve fractional personhood, he went on, "we should allow representation to oxen, horses & c."[20]

In the mid-1840s slaveholders had reason to feel confident about the future of the "peculiar institution." In early 1845, just before the Louisiana legislators convened, Florida had been admitted to the Union as a slave state, while Congress had voted to permit the Republic of Texas to accede to the Union, where it might serve as the basis for as many as four slave states. Yet Benjamin, worldly and far-seeing, recognized that anti-slavery sentiment was gathering force in the North. Soon, he told his colleagues, the threat to slavery would reduce the squabbles of Whig and Democrat to idle chatter. "That man must be indeed blind not to perceive from whence the danger comes. . . . The course of events within the last few months proves that we must rely upon ourselves and our Southern confederates to maintain our rights and cause them to be respected, and not upon the stipulations in the Federal compact." The implication, that the current party system would give way to one opposing slave-holders to abolitionists, was still a decade in the future.

Benjamin recited none of the classical justifications of slav-ery; in that setting, of course, he hardly needed to do so. But he almost always avoided the ugly question of treating a class of humans as property; here, as elsewhere, he cast himself as the defender of the existing order. That posture came naturally to him, for Benjamin was a conservative in both the doctrinal and the temperamental sense. Though he favored a modest exten-sion of the franchise, he opposed a proposal to elect, rather than appoint, judges, as well as the secretary of state. He en-dorsed efforts to make the constitution harder to amend. He supported a provision that would require four years of resi-dency to be eligible to serve in the General Assembly, as a bul-wark against Northern immigrants bearing Northern princi-ples. Even his support for mandatory public schooling had a preservationist flavor. "Unless means were taken to enlighten the masses," he declared, "in order that they may be enabled to exercise political rights, with the extreme opinions which now prevail, it requires no great foresight to predict that we shall soon reach a state of complete anarchy."[21]

The New Orleans to which Benjamin had moved as a very young man was a remote outpost of a nation still gathered along the Eastern Seaboard; but by the time he established himself as one of the city's leading figures, his home town was well on its way to becoming one of America's great cities. A vast inflow of

Irish and German immigrants swelled the population of New Orleans from 46,000 in 1830 to 168,000 thirty years later, tying it with Baltimore as the nation's second-largest city after New York. Men like Benjamin, or the Slidell brothers, or Benjamin's cousin, Henry Hyams, who would become the state's lieutenant governor, had come from outside New Orleans and increasingly looked beyond its confines.

In 1847, Benjamin was asked to serve as counsel to the California Land Commission, which was charged with settling land claims after the United States seized the territory in the early stages of the war with Mexico. For the first time, he saw the West. After Zachary Taylor, a Whig, was elected president in 1848, Benjamin went to Washington to mingle with the new ruling team. It was later said that Taylor planned to offer Benjamin a cabinet post but was dissuaded after he heard scandalous tales of Natalie. Nevertheless, the visit had offered Benjamin a tantalizing whiff of national power.

The need to integrate New Orleans into the national economy offered new business opportunities, and Benjamin did his best to seize them. The South had fallen far behind the North in the building of railroads, and thus continued to rely on waterways. New Orleans itself depended on the Mississippi and a system of local canals. In the early 1840s, Benjamin had joined a group of local businessmen calling for a rail link between New Orleans and Jackson, Mississippi. In 1850, he was retained by P. A. Hargous, a New York investor who had signed an agreement with the Mexican government to build a railroad across the Tehuantepec isthmus, a vast undertaking that would have linked the Atlantic and Pacific, as the Panama Canal later did. Benjamin served as legal counsel but also as the company's publicist. He undertook this task with the same relish he brought to the courtroom. In 1852, speaking at the Southwestern Railroad Convention, he asked his listeners to imagine a railroad running from New Orleans north to Jackson, and thence across the Tehuantepec. "What have we before us?" Benjamin cried, according to a local newspaper account. "The Eastern world! Its commerce makes empires of the countries to which it flows, and when they are deprived of it they are as empty bags, useless, valueless. That commerce belongs to New Orleans."[22] Benjamin would pursue this empire-building dream, and the stupendous wealth that would have come with it, for much of the next decade.

Benjamin's legal practice continued to grow, and to expose him to a world beyond New Orleans and Louisiana. In 1848 he was admitted to the bar of the U.S. Supreme Court; over the ensuing decade he would appear before the High Court more often than any other Southern attorney save Reverdy Johnson, a famed jurist from Maryland. In his very first case, Benjamin began to speak only half an hour before the noon recess and said that he would do no more than present the facts of the case. One of the justices later told Senator George Graham Vest of Missouri that "he had never listened in all his experience to a statement so lucid, comprehensive and convincing," and warned opposing counsel, "You had better look to your laurels, for that little Jew from New Orleans has stated your case out of court." At five foot six, Benjamin was not particularly "little"; the justice may have thought of Jews generally as making up in guile what they lacked in stature. Such casual epithets then passed for harmless raillery rather than actual bigotry. The fact that Vest ascribed this remark to "Justice Field," presumably meaning Stephen Field, who did not begin serving until 1863, raises some question about the accuracy of his memory.[23] But the story Vest told comported with the general view of Benjamin.

Even as his stature grew, Benjamin suffered a painful reversal. In 1852, a flood wiped out his entire cane crop. At the same time, an associate whose $60,000 loan he had agreed to guarantee defaulted, and Benjamin had to repay the bank. He was forced to sell his half-share of the plantation to Theodore Pack-wood. Such was the value of both the physical plant and the human capital—that is, the slaves—that Packwood paid Benjamin $168,000 for his share. (The sum is equivalent to $5 million today.) He moved Rebecca and Leah to a house outside town, and moved in with a friend on Polymnia Street at the edge of the Garden District, where he had once disdained to live. Benjamin had regarded the plantation as the irrefutable evidence of his exalted standing. His social life, his family life, his budding career as a progressive agriculturalist, had all been centered there. Now it was gone. But starting over was second nature to him.

In any case, Benjamin was already so deeply rooted in New Orleans' social order that he no longer needed Bellechasse to establish his bona fides. He had been admitted to the Boston Club, which had been founded in 1841 by "thirty leading mercantile and professional men of the city" who devoted their evenings to Boston, a card game like whist. It constituted the apex of the social hierarchy, at least among Americans.[24] Benjamin was the first Jewish member. As an avid and talented card player, he must have been especially welcome. Benjamin had come to be viewed as a man who knew how to do everything correctly—try a case, serve a roast, address a lady, deal a hand. A friend, Samuel Barlow, wrote from New York to complain that he couldn't get proper coffee. "Poor untaught savages of New York!" Benjamin wrote back in his usual rallying spirit. He then proceeded to instruct Barlow in the proper brewing of coffee—one-third mocha to two-thirds java, allow ten to fifteen minutes for steeping, etc. Benjamin allowed that he had "strong doubts" about Barlow's own recipe for hot lemonade, and closed by saying that he was overwhelmed with court appearances, none involving disputes of less than $100,000.[25] With the very obvious exception of his family life, Benjamin, barely forty, had achieved a masterful ease in New Orleans society.

His ambitions, however, were not slaked. Benjamin's service in the state legislature and two constitutional conventions
had made him one of the state's leading Whigs. In 1851, he ran
for the Whig nomination for the U.S. Senate. Whigs outnumbered Democrats in the state, so the party contest would determine the ultimate winner. Benjamin was not the favorite. The
New Orleans *Delta*, then the city's chief paper, praised him in
decidedly ambiguous language, though without ever alluding
to his religious faith.

> His boyish figure and girlish face—his gentle, innocent, in-
> genuous expression and manner—his sweet and beautifully
> modulated voice, would render him decidedly the most un-
> senatorial figure in that body of gray heads and full grown
> men. But when he should arise in the Senate, and in the most
> modest and graceful manner proceed to pour forth a strain
> of the most fluent and beautifully expressed ideas . . . then
> would the old senators stretch their eyes and mouths with
> wonder, whispering to one another, "That's a devilish smart
> little fellow."[26]

The editors insisted that the state needed Benjamin too much
to send him to Washington. But they didn't know that John
Slidell, now the state's Democratic boss, had lined up support
for Benjamin through his own network. Benjamin won the
nomination on the second ballot. New Orleans had served as a
booster in the rocket bearing Benjamin aloft; like Charleston,
it fell away as he reached greater heights.

3

❖◗◆◖❖

Washington

THE WHIG PARTY that Judah Benjamin represented was coming apart at the seams as he arrived in Washington in early 1853. The shared belief in a modern manufacturing economy, an active national government, and a high-minded Protestant moralism could not hold together men who were divided on the question of slavery. The steady expansion of the nation westward had forced the issue of slavery into national debate, for the admission of each new state threatened to upset the balance between free and slave states. In 1850, Henry Clay, the Great Compromiser of 1820, had just barely cobbled together a deal that allowed the admission of California and New Mexico as free states in exchange for strict enforcement of the Fugitive Slave Act, which in turn outraged Northern opinion. Northern Whigs began to abandon the party, while Southern members considered decamping for the Democrats or the anti-immigrant but pro-Union American Party, known as the Know Nothings.[1]

The fierce debate in the first half of 1854 over the Kansas-Nebraska Act, which demonstrated that the tenuous terms of 1850 could no longer hold, forced Benjamin to reconsider his own affiliation. In June he wrote to a Virginia Whig to report that a visit to New York had left him feeling that "a gulf wide, deep and, I fear, impassable" had opened between Northern and Southern Whigs. Pro-slavery nationalists needed to form a new party made up of Southern Whigs and "the National wing of the Democratic party in the North"—just as he had forecast a decade earlier.[2] He would not cast his lot with the nativists, as others had. In the 1840s Benjamin had endorsed the kind of restrictions on citizenship now favored by the American Party. But he recoiled at Know-Nothing intolerance and obscurantism. In an 1855 newspaper interview, he explained that he had repudiated the party "because they are anti-republican in refusing equal political rights to all American citizens; because they violate the spirit, if not the very letter, of the American Constitution, by the proscription of citizens on the grounds of their religious beliefs."[3] Benjamin wrote, of course, as a patriotic American rather than a Jew; no one could accuse him of special pleading.

By the summer of 1855, Benjamin had given up altogether on his own party, and had begun rousing Southerners to the imminent dangers of a new Republican party in the grip of abolitionism. In a letter to the New Orleans *Delta*, Benjamin illustrated the gross injustice of the anti-slavery agitation with a hypothetical that must have greatly amused him. "Suppose," he wrote, "a body of insane fanatics in this section of the Confederacy should avow their belief in the sinfulness of subjecting the animal creation to the domination and service of man." Suppose further that they "organize bands of robbers and incendiaries" to steal Northern flocks. Suppose that Southern legislatures actually protected such scoundrels. How long would the North put up with it? No longer, of course, than the South should be expected to tolerate abolitionist fanatics.[4] This sort of ingenious rhetorical exercise had always served Benjamin well in the courthouse.

Benjamin first entered the raging debate over slavery with a skillful cross-examination. In July 1854, Senator Charles Sumner, one of the chamber's leading abolitionists, delivered a speech denouncing the Fugitive Slave Act, which permitted masters to pursue and capture their slaves in free states. Sumner, a vehement orator given to the hyperbolic turn of phrase, called the law both unjust and unconstitutional. Abolitionists had begun to read the Constitution in an anti-slavery light; nevertheless, the so-called fugitive slave clause required "a person held to service or labor" who flees across state lines to be returned to his master. Benjamin rose and addressed a series of questions to his honorable colleague from Massachusetts.

After first reading out the Constitution's all-too-plain language, Benjamin asked Sumner whether he believed the clause to apply to slaves. The latter, apparently flummoxed, resorted to flattery in order to avoid giving an answer. "The manner of the Senator from Louisiana," Sumner intoned, "is always so kind and so much in conformity with the proprieties of debate that I shall have great pleasure in answering his question; but I should prefer to wait until he gets through." Benjamin responded that he *had* gotten through; he just wanted an answer to his question. Having no good answer, Sumner tried to change the subject by asking Benjamin whether the Fugitive Slave Act would permit South Carolina to imprison a visiting free black— perhaps a reference to the state's Negro Seaman Act of 1822, which authorized the temporary detention of free black sailors. After dismissing the idea out of hand, the Louisiana senator provoked laughter by saying, "This is a very extraordinary way of answering a question." After another exchange, and more circumlocution, Benjamin said triumphantly, "My object is answered, sir."[5] That is, Sumner had no answer. Benjamin had demonstrated to his colleagues that his reputation as a first-rate lawyer was well deserved.

Sumner, of course, soon became famous as the victim of a far less decorous exchange. After he had delivered a five-hour anti-slavery harangue in May 1856, Senator Preston Brooks of South Carolina attacked him with a cane and came very close to murdering his colleague. This was only the most notorious battle of a bloody war, of words and weapons, in both the House and the Senate.

The fundamentally irreconcilable nature of the debate over slavery and the growing mutual hatred of North and South set legislators against one another in a kind of premonitory civil war. Members routinely accused one another of lying. South-erners regularly challenged Northerners to a duel, knowing full well that the latter considered dueling a species of Southern barbarity. Eventually the Northern members began fighting back, culminating in an astonishing slugfest pitting squads from both sides against one another on February 6, 1858. The *Charles-ton Mercury* singled out this donnybrook as the most conse-quential of all the Capitol brawls, for it was "a sectional and not a personal quarrel. It was North against South."[6]

The giants of yore—Clay, Calhoun, Webster, Adams—no longer strode the halls of Congress. These were not only lesser men, but far more partisan ones. Very few Southern legislators enjoyed the respect of Northern members during this period; but Benjamin did. He was an emollient figure who could ad-vance the Southern cause without provoking his rivals to fury or casting obvious aspersions on their character. His lawyer's dispassion never deserted him; he applied the language of sweet reason even when he intended to draw blood, as he did with Sumner. Perhaps he simply hid his feelings more effectively than other men did. Sumner may have been flattering his col-league only in order to buy himself time, but others really did regard Benjamin as a gentleman. After a long speech in which

Benjamin denounced the Kansas-Nebraska Act, Senator John P. Hale of New Hampshire said that he had listened "with great pleasure as I always do, on account of his acknowledged ability, his great eloquence, his very persuasive powers, his mellifluous voice, his winning and graceful manner." All that, Hale added, "only makes me regret that he is in a wrong position."[7]

Yet Benjamin's Jewishness made him a target as well. In the midst of the violent debate over the extension of slavery to Kansas, the abolitionist Benjamin Wade ingeniously described Benjamin as a Jewish version of a "doughface," the notorious gibe that the Virginian John Randolph had directed at spineless Northerners who supported the slave power. When Moses led the enslaved people of Israel out of Egypt, Wade cried, "I suppose that Pharaoh and all the chivalry of old Egypt denounced him as a most furious abolitionist. . . . They were not exactly Northern men with Southern principles; they were Israelites with Egyptian principles." That must have hit home. Legend has it that Benjamin retorted that when his ancestors were receiving the Decalogue from God, Wade's "were herding swine in the forests of Great Britain."[8]

Benjamin was in fact a rather exotic creature in Washington; a quarter century in the rarefied Creole society of New Orleans had made him into the kind of worldly, and distinctly feminized, gentleman likelier to be found in the pages of Stendhal than the hallways of the Capitol. Whatever loneliness or humiliation he felt from Natalie's abandonment and the loss of his only child, Benjamin wore in public an air of perfect urbanity. Thomas Bayard, scion of a Delaware political dynasty and later a senator himself, recalled Benjamin's "half smile . . . that sometimes seemed to degenerate into a simper"—that drawing-room politesse that verged on ingratiating hypocrisy. "To my mother and young daughters at tea-tables he was an ever-welcome guest," Bayard wrote, "and as a consummate player of whist, he was equally companionable to my father."[9]

Benjamin certainly had male friends, including Bayard and David Yulee of Florida, the other Jew, or part-Jew, of the Senate; but the great friend of his life, as well as his most penetrating observer, was Varina Davis. The two first met in the spring of 1853, when Benjamin was invited to dinner at the White House by President Franklin Pierce. Varina was the twenty-six-year-old wife of Jefferson Davis, Pierce's secretary of war; she had had the rare good fortune among women of her world to be taught literature and philosophy when young, and never doubted her intellectual equality with the men around her—though she was careful about demonstrating that equality.

At that first encounter, Varina observed that Benjamin spoke only of trifles: "He had rather the air of a witty bon vivant than that of a great Senator." Physically, she noted, "his type was decidedly Hebrew; he had not a marked line in his face, which was boyish in the extreme, and was rendered more so by soft black curls about his temple and forehead."[10] Varina was so struck by Benjamin's startling youthfulness that, when she recalled this meeting in a letter written long afterward, she recorded his age as thirty-one, a decade shy of the truth. Yet by the end of the decade, the South would look to Benjamin as an indomitable champion of its cause.

The legislative compromises that had forestalled the issue of slavery depended on a wish to avoid conflict that was swiftly evaporating by the middle of the 1850s. In 1854, Senator Stephen A. Douglas, Democrat of Illinois, submitted the Kansas-Nebraska Act, which proposed to eliminate the Missouri Compromise in favor of the doctrine of "popular sovereignty," leaving to the people of the new state the decision whether or not to permit slavery. Many Northerners, both Whig and Democrat, had come to regard the Missouri Compromise as the guarantee that slavery would not spread beyond the South. Southerners, who objected to the Missouri Compromise for the same reason, had come around to support Douglas's bill only when he had agreed to language eliminating Clay's famous handiwork. Though Kansas-Nebraska passed the Senate, it remained stalled in the House. Settlers pouring into Kansas from both North and South turned the territory into a tinderbox of political struggle and guerrilla violence. "Free-soil" settlers from the North formed a self-proclaimed territorial government to rival the official one that pro-slave Missourians had dominated thanks to shameless abuse and intimidation at the ballot box. Both sought recognition from Congress as the legitimate voice of Kansas.

By 1856 it had become clear that free-soilers would soon greatly outnumber pro-slave forces; any result consistent with "popular sovereignty" would lead to the prohibition of slavery. Judah Benjamin now helped lead the charge against the very principle Southerners had accepted two years before. In a speech in May 1856, he declared, as John Calhoun had in debates over "nullification" a generation earlier, that the Constitution was a pact not among individual citizens but between "the free and independent states which that instrument links together in a common bond of union." If, Benjamin went on, sovereignty ultimately inhered in the states, how could any new territory "be used according to the principles of the North to the exclusion of the South"? States, of course, could choose to permit slavery or not, but no territory could prejudge that decision by voting to exclude slaves, and thus slaveholders. If Benjamin had still adhered to the *Somerset* principle that slavery could exist only by dint of positive law, he would have had to conclude that new territories were born free. But that was a long-ago moment of advocacy. Benjamin now denied that slavery violated the order of nature. He did not claim, as Southerners increasingly did, that slavery was an affirmative good for slaves as well as masters. Rather, he insisted that slavery and free-soil constituted different economic choices, not different moral orders. The South accepted the North's choice; why couldn't the North do the same? Why must the North seek to bring the whole nation beneath its yoke?

And the South? Its cause was not slavery as such, but "property, honor, safety." The property, of course, was the $2 billion in human chattels. Honor was at stake because slavery was the Southern way of life. And safety was threatened "because our property, now kept in proper subjection, peaceful and laborious, would be converted into an idle, reckless, criminal population, led on to their foul purpose by inflamed passions." This was a trump card that Benjamin often played; perhaps he had never forgotten the terrifying night when Charleston trembled before Denmark Vesey and his band. Now he reminded his colleagues of the yet more terrifying example of the slave rebellion in Haiti. "We cannot," he declared, "be ignorant of the fate that awaits us"—butchery and rape. Benjamin dramatically announced that he could no longer remain a member of the Whig party; he was leaving for the Democrats, whom he still hoped to convert to Unionism. Yet he asserted, in a rafter-raising peroration, that the need to defend property, honor, and safety might preempt Union:

> Yes sir, let the note of alarm be sounded throughout the land; let the people only be informed; let them be told of the momentous crisis which is at hand; and they will rise in their might, and placing their heel on the head of the serpent that has glided into their Eden, they will crush it to the earth, once and forever.[11]

That sounded very much like a call to arms. Benjamin's early biographers nevertheless excused his eloquent defense of the unspeakable by describing him as a moderate in an immoderate time. "If Benjamin was not one of the rare men who would sacrifice his political future and stand against the crowd," wrote Robert Douthat Meade in 1943, neither was he an extremist.

"On the slavery question he was too conservative; he stood for the *status quo* and had not yet offered any satisfactory solution to the internecine problem." Yet Benjamin "knew the Negro" as the fire-eating abolitionists did not. "What a pity abolition could not have been planned and administered with the help of men like him!"[12]

This is absurd; abolition could have been "planned and administered" only if the South had agreed to surrender the practice voluntarily, which it would not have done. It is true that Benjamin's language was temperate compared with his more venomous colleagues; slavery for him was a necessary and profitable practice rather than a holy cause. Benjamin may well have been a relatively benevolent slave-master, as his first biographer, Pierce Butler, concludes; yet he was pleased to make an analogy between abolitionism and the fanciful belief that beasts must be released from servitude. How, then, are we to think of him?

Judah Benjamin was, as we shall see, a brave man; but his courage was of the sort that belongs to survivors, not saints. And Meade was surely right in saying that Benjamin would have had to draw upon a deep fund of moral courage in order to repudiate the Southern way of life. Earlier in the century, when slavery was not threatened, Southerners, at least in the border states, had often expressed qualms about the practice, and even ventured to hope that slaves might be peacefully emancipated and then returned to Africa. But by the time Benjamin had become a public figure, even the most modest skepticism over slavery had been deemed unacceptable in the Deep South and had thus become unaffordable to a man of ambition. The moral courage that one finds in figures like John Quincy Adams or Joshua Reed Giddings, an Ohio congressman expelled for goading the South on slavery, or in abolitionists like Theodore Dwight Weld, has little equivalent in the South (unless one counts the readiness to martyr oneself on the altar of "states' rights," as the slaveholders themselves would).

Our instinct to hold Judah Benjamin to a higher standard because he was a Jew ignores the near-universal ownership of slaves among Southern Jews of means, not to mention the unwillingness of Southern Jews to rock the boat in which they sailed to a life of prosperity and freedom. Even Northern Jews hesitated to do so. The authors of an American and Foreign Anti-Slavery Society report in 1853 asked why the "Jews of the United States have never taken any steps whatever with regard to the Slavery question." The answer: "As citizens, they deem it their policy 'to have everyone choose which ever side he may deem best to promote his own interests and the welfare of his country.'" That was a fair-minded summation, for Jews were as divided as Christians on the question of slavery. Some Reform Jews were ardent abolitionists, while others were not. Jewish businessmen and laborers who depended on trade with the South typically sided with the Democrats against the anti-slavery Republicans. Others found sanction for slavery in the Old Testament. In a celebrated address in New York on January 4, 1861, Orthodox Rabbi Morris Jacob Raphall argued that slavery had existed before the flood and was nowhere outlawed either in the Mosaic code or even in the New Testament. "How are you denouncing slaveholding as a sin?" he thundered at abolitionist Henry Ward Beecher. Raphall insisted that the coming war could be avoided if only both North and South accepted the biblical practice of according slaves rights "not conflicting with the rights of his master."[13]

If anything distinguished Benjamin from those around him, it was his *knowledge*. He "knew the Negro," as Meade says—knew from daily life in New Orleans that racial distinctions were more social than biological, knew from the plantation that black men could do the same work as whites. He admitted as much in the *Creole* case, in which he had defended escaped slaves. Benjamin was also a worldly, well-traveled man who could not take refuge in Southern parochialism. In the Paris salons he often visited, slavery was held to be an inhuman practice. Benjamin subscribed to the *Revue des Deux Mondes*, the journal that published France's leading thinkers—Ernest Renan, Théophile Gautier, Alexandre Dumas. He kept up with the magazine even during the Civil War years. In 1864, he would admit to a correspondent, who favored freeing the slaves as part of the war effort, that in the pages of the *Revue*, "abolitionist sentiments are quietly assumed as philosophical axioms too self-evident to require comment or elaboration." Benjamin knew that the thinkers he most admired would have sneered at his own arguments.[14]

Such willful blindness, to be sure, is hardly extraordinary. In *The Subjection of Women*, his truly heroic act of identification with an oppressed class to which he did not belong, John Stuart Mill rhetorically asks, "Was there ever any domination that did not seem natural to those who possessed it?" Mill observes that even Aristotle, the greatest of thinkers, justified slavery. Writing in 1869, Mill notes that we need scarcely revert to ancient thinkers to find that the great advantages produced by mastery blind the beneficiaries to its true nature. "Did not the slave-owners of the Southern United States maintain the same doctrine," he asks, "with all the fanaticism with which men cling to the theories that justify their passions and legitimate their personal interests?"[15] Only the rare man refuses to accept a theory upon which all the conveniences of his life rest. Mill was such a man; Judah Benjamin was not. It is also true, however, that by 1869 Mill was revered as the foremost thinker in England, whereas Benjamin, whatever his reputation, always understood that as a Jew he stood on shaky ground. Apostasy, in his case, would have carried the terrible price of exile.

Benjamin's reputation as one of the South's most talented and lavishly recompensed lawyers had preceded him to Washington. In the fall of 1852, President Millard Fillmore, a fellow

Whig, had asked Benjamin to serve on the Supreme Court, which of course would have made him the first Jew to do so. Benjamin declined; he probably would have been bored on the bench. Besides, he had no intention of terminating an immensely lucrative legal career. When Benjamin arrived in Washington, lawmakers received $8 per diem (though in 1855 the figure would rise to a more livable $3,000 annually). Many legislators supplemented their income with private work; few could rival the $40,000 to $50,000 Benjamin averaged from his ongoing legal practice. Benjamin was not shy about using his political contacts to advance his burgeoning business career. He spent the long annual recesses back in Louisiana representing corporate clients; he traveled extensively both in the United States and abroad, including annual trips to Paris to see Natalie and Ninette, whom he continued to support.

Even before joining the Senate, Benjamin had lobbied the administration of President Fillmore to support the so-called Hargous-Garay grant to build a trans-isthmian rail line. (Garay was the Mexican partner of the investor Hargous.) In Fillmore's final days, in early March 1853, American diplomats had signed a treaty recognizing a rival grant from a Colonel Sloo; but the new president, Franklin Pierce, refused either to accept the treaty or to intervene on Benjamin's behalf. In June 1856, Benjamin received a letter from a State Department official tartly observing that recent discussions had "put a different light on the Sloo grant from what you presented," and stating that the Pierce administration would not intervene in a private matter.[16]

That fall, James Buchanan, a Pennsylvania Democrat prepared to adopt the Southern view on territorial expansion and the Fugitive Slave Act, became president with the critical support of John Slidell, Benjamin's old friend and political mentor and now the junior senator from Louisiana. Slidell had brought Benjamin into the campaign as well. Once taking office, Buchanan surrounded himself with leading Southern figures both in government and among his circle of close advisers. Benjamin had a friend in the White House, and thus became the central figure in efforts to win political support for the Hargous grant.

Thanks to a surviving cache of letters between himself and Hargous (preserved by the latter), we hear the usually masterful Benjamin trying to manage the expectations he had raised. On April 2, a month after the new president had been sworn in, Hargous wrote to Benjamin to say that he expected "a dispatch from you stating that *all is right*." But everything was not all right. In early July Benjamin informed Hargous that he had just spoken to President Buchanan, who had imparted the shocking news that the administration would endorse neither grant, leaving both teams to recuperate the funds they had given to Mexican authorities. "I begged the president," Benjamin wrote, "to withhold the instructions he had already prepared to give me a chance to write all the parties. . . . After some hesitation, he consented."

Now the gambler in Benjamin emerged. The time had come, the Louisiana senator went on, for a bold move: drop the bid and join forces with the Sloo team, working together to recoup the lost funds. Benjamin promised to surrender his own equity, cushioning the loss for others, in order to help reach a fifty-fifty deal with the Sloo party. Hargous must have found this an appealing proposition. He agreed, and offered the lawyer-legislator a 5 percent commission instead. Benjamin went back to work pulling strings in Washington. Secretary of State Lewis Cass dispatched a note to John Forsyth, the American minister in Mexico, asking him to support the venture.[17]

Benjamin now proceeded to negotiate with the Sloo team, draft the new corporation documents, issue stock and bonds, and prepare to leave for Mexico with $4,500 from Hargous. He reached Mexico City in August 1857. After years of working in the southwest, Benjamin spoke excellent Spanish, and he went to work on the nation's senior political leaders. On August 30 Benjamin was able to report to Hargous that the government had agreed to nullify the Sloo grant and to accept Tehuantepec, to offer a sixty-year concession, to take a smaller cut of profits than planned, and so on. President Ignacio Comonfort, the very temporary occupant of a presidential carousel, had approved the transaction. "I consider the charter worth millions more than the old one," Benjamin exulted. Two weeks later, back in New Orleans, he gave Hargous a long account of his triumphs over interference from Washington and demands from the Sloo backers. He had, he added, given a complete account to President Buchanan.

Benjamin never wanted to expose the discipline and effort required to advance his vast ambitions. Hidden beneath his amiability and his Creolized elegance were the furious labors of the promoter—the relentless lobbying, the threats and promises, the mastery of fine print, the unsinkable optimism in the face of endless obstacles. Benjamin didn't have the money; he worked for the man who did. It was he who now raised funds from investors; re-negotiated the agreement with a new Mexican president, Benito Juárez; and persuaded the postmaster of California to route the mails through Tehuantepec, providing an important source of potential revenue for the proposed railroad. What had begun as a gleam in the eye of P. A. Hargous a decade earlier finally began to take on reality. The company sent engineers to survey the property in early 1859. The lay of the land, the navigability of the rivers—all seemed propitious. Benjamin stood to finally make his fortune.

Then, in May 1859, Hargous Brothers of New York went bankrupt. Benjamin tried to raise funds elsewhere, including from the Mexican government; but the Civil War cut short his plans. The railroad would never be built; perhaps, given the harsh terrain, never fully explored, it could not have been. In the National Archives Robert Douthat Meade found a black bank box belonging to Benjamin that contained $29,000 of worthless bonds in the Tehuantepec railroad, $94,000 in stock, and a note promising him a $45,000 commission upon the first bond issue.[18]

Benjamin had evidently carried the box with him to Richmond, the capital of the Confederacy, and left it there when he fled.

For all his wealth, Judah Benjamin lived simply in Washington, renting several rooms in a private home on F Street between Thirteenth and Fourteenth, an area very popular with members of the Senate. He dined at a "mess" nearby with other Southern congressmen who lived alone, as he did. (The Free-Soilers and Republicans, according to a leading hostess of the day, kept to the other side of the street.) In 1859, however, Benjamin made an extraordinary decision: he would bring Natalie to the city from Paris. Natalie barely recalled English, knew nothing of the rigid decorum that governed Washington society, and was rumored to conduct frequent affairs. Benjamin could not have thought that Natalie was any more concerned with his own reputation than she had been when she had abandoned him fifteen years before; but he may have believed that she would relent now that he could place at her feet everything she had ever dreamed of. And before whom, if not her, could he indulge the pride he felt at having attained the highest possible social standing?

With the same fatal instinct that had once led him to purchase Bellechasse, Benjamin rented the most storied private home in Washington: the Decatur House, looking straight across Lafayette Square at the White House. This three-story square brick house had been built by America's first architect, Benjamin Latrobe, for the naval hero Stephen Decatur. There Decatur had famously bled to death after a duel. Subsequent tenants included the French ambassador, Hyde de Neuville, Martin Van Buren, and Henry Clay. The Decatur House had a vaulted entrance hall and a splendid grand staircase. By the 1850s, however, the owners had begun renting out rooms, and the house had become a patchwork. The disrepair offered Benjamin the opportunity to remodel and refurbish the house top to bottom. From Washington's finest galleries and shops he purchased paintings and *objets d'art*, furniture and china, silver and crystal. He prepared the house as if for the arrival of a princess.[19] Natalie herself is said to have attended the auction of King Louis Philippe's furnishings at the Tuileries, and to have shipped several choice items to Washington.[20]

Tales of Natalie's louche life had, unfortunately, reached Washington, and once she arrived, in 1859, the wives of the leading Southern senators met to determine whether a visit would be deemed correct. Virginia Clay-Clopton, wife of Alabama senator Clement Clay, later recounted in her gossip-filled memoir, *Belle of the Fifties*, that her husband had tipped the scales, observing, "You have nothing to do with the lady's private life, and, as a mark of esteem to a statesman of her husband's prominence, it will be better to call." One day when Mrs. Benjamin was receiving, Mrs. Clay-Clopton writes, the ladies went in caravan, "paid our devoirs to the hostess, and retired." Having left their calling cards, they waited for the obligatory return visit. None occurred; Mrs. Benjamin made no effort to socialize with her peers. Benjamin's colleague John Slidell lived across the square, and Natalie would likely have befriended his aristocratic Creole wife, Mathilde Deslonde. Tales circulated of splendid gatherings organized for French diplomats.

Two months later, Natalie disappeared—for a rendezvous, rumor had it, with a German officer. Every splendid article with which Benjamin had filled the Decatur House was now sold at auction. "Everyone in Washington now thronged to see the beautiful things," writes Mrs. Clay-Clopton, rather in glee than in lamentation.[21] Senator David Yulee of Florida, like Benjamin a non-professing Jew from the Caribbean and Charleston and one of his few close friends in Washington, bought many of the most beautiful pieces—out of pity, presumably, rather than covetousness. It is barely possible to imagine the shame, the anger, the remorse, Benjamin must have felt. How had a man so prudent, so acutely sensitive to his own precarious standing, placed himself, yet again, in so humiliating a position? He must have found the sympathy of his friends, and of his alleged friends, unbearable. Benjamin left Washington during the auction, and only reluctantly returned at all. Rather than move back to F Street, he took rooms at the Old Washington Club on Madison Place, across Lafayette Park from the scene of his disaster.

The death knell of the Union was sounded on March 6, 1857, when the Supreme Court handed down its decision in the *Dred Scott* case. Had the Court merely confirmed the constitutionality of the fugitive slave laws by holding that a slave remained his master's property even once he had reached a free state, the North would have been outraged, but scarcely shocked. But the Court went on to assert that Congress did not have the authority to prohibit slavery in a territory, thus invalidating the Missouri Compromise and the logic that had enabled the negotiated admission of new states. Until that moment, the Democrats had been divided between advocates of "popular sovereignty" and those, like Benjamin, who demanded the unfettered right to bring slaves into new territories. That argument was now settled. Republicans, on the other hand, concluded that all three branches of government had fallen into the clutches of the Slave Power. Republicans stood for the principle that Charles Sumner had encapsulated in a speech in 1852: "freedom national, slavery sectional." This was the principle of *Somerset*. *Dred Scott* threatened to reverse those terms—to make slavery "the common patrimony and shame of all the States," as the journalist William Cullen Bryant acidly put it.[22]

The congressional session of 1857–58 was convulsed with debates over Kansas and *Dred Scott*. Nothing said there settled anything; the goal was no longer to find common ground, or even to win over wavering moderates, but rather for each side to demonstrate the self-evident truth of its position. Benjamin joined the debate with a lengthy speech in March 1858 that served as an erudite refutation of the principles of *Somerset*. Had not Queen Elizabeth owned slaves? Had not Charles II granted royal charters permitting the practice? The English common law under which the charters of the colonies had been framed "regarded slaves as chattels." Slavery was national—global—and freedom local. Congress thus had no right to prohibit slavery in a territory.[23]

Benjamin had thrown himself into the cause of the South; yet an episode now occurred that implied that the feelings were not quite reciprocal. In the course of debate in June 1858, Benjamin said that he did not believe the secretary of war had asked Congress for funding for "breech-loading arms." Jefferson Davis, senator from Mississippi and himself a former secretary of war, as well as a revered military figure, instantly contradicted him. Davis must have sardonically implied that a civilian like Benjamin had no business discussing weaponry, for the latter objected to Davis's "sneering reply." The exchange quickly degenerated:

> "If the Senator finds it disagreeable, I hope he will keep it to himself."
> "When directed to me, I will not keep it to myself; I will repel it instanter."
> "You have got it, sir."
> "That is enough, sir."

Davis made matters much worse when he was heard to mutter about "the arguments of a paid attorney"—an unmistakable gibe from a genteel planter to a man of commerce. Benjamin, who may have also divined the unspoken word "Jew" in Davis's insult, asked if he had heard correctly, and Davis confirmed that he had. Benjamin immediately wrote out a challenge and asked his friend Senator James Bayard to deliver it to Davis in the Senate cloakroom.[24]

What in the world was this about? Benjamin was one of the most peaceable men in the Senate, and in any case he and Davis were on the same side. The animosity seems to have come from Davis. Varina Davis later reflected that "they were too much alike, in many respects, to be at first very good friends." Varina was thinking of their "tireless mental energy," their "nervously excitable tempers," their ambition.[25] Yet in most respects these two men, who would soon become not just very good friends but almost a conjoined pair at the heart of the Confederacy, were not at all alike. It would be more accurate to say that each ultimately found something indispensable in the other.

Davis was a son of the soil, born in a Kentucky log cabin like the man who would become the adversary of his life, Abraham Lincoln. A Westerner could become either a Southerner or a Northerner, depending on where he moved: the Lincolns went north, and the Davises south and farther west, to Mississippi. Davis never had the grace of manner of Tidewater aristocrats like Robert E. Lee, later his classmate at West Point. Perhaps in this regard he found himself an outsider in elevated Southern circles, as Benjamin did. Yet the center of gravity of the South was moving from the tobacco plantations of Virginia to the cotton belt along the Mississippi. Davis was, as one of his biographers puts it, a scion of the new South.[26]

After West Point, Davis was sent to the frontier, where he fell in love with Sarah Knox Taylor, the daughter of General Zachary Taylor. Since the general would not permit his daughter to marry a military man, Davis, though every inch a soldier, resigned his military commission and married Sarah. Three months later, she died of malaria. Davis was already a solemn figure very much in the grip of the Southern code of honor; now he was plunged into grief. His much older brother, Joseph, had become one of the new rich of the Mississippi, and gave Jefferson a five-hundred-acre slice of his vast plantation. There he lingered, solitary, for eight years. In 1844 he was introduced to the seventeen-year-old Varina Howell, a well-born, well-educated, and exceptionally intelligent child of Natchez society. In a letter to her mother, Varina said that she couldn't tell if the thirty-five-year-old widower was young or old—"he looks both at times." He was, she said tellingly, "the kind of person I should expect to rescue me from a mad dog at any risk, but to insist upon a stoical indifference to the fright afterwards."[27]

Marriage to Varina restored Davis to life. He volunteered for the army when the Mexican War broke out and won lasting fame when he led his men to victory at the Battle of Buena Vista. At the end he had to be helped off his horse, his boot filled with blood. The war made Davis a martial hero with a grandiose conception of his gifts as a leader of men. But he was unable to walk without crutches for the next two years; for the rest of his life he lived in terrible pain from a combination of physical and nervous ailments.[28] Leadership and suffering would henceforth be joined in his mind.

Davis was a zealot of states' rights in the mold of John Calhoun. "There is no sovereignty inherent in that entity known as the United States of America," he wrote.[29] So stern were his principles that Davis refused to accept a promotion from President James Knox Polk on the grounds that he had accepted an appointment in a state militia, over which the federal government had no constitutional authority. As a plantation owner and a Christian, Davis entertained no doubt that God had granted the white man sovereignty over "the dusky sons of Ham," but his ardor was aroused less by the defense of slavery than by the rising nationalism of the new South. The territorial gains from the Mexican War had rendered the idea of a self-sustaining Southern nation increasingly plausible.

Elected to the Senate from Mississippi in 1847, Davis became a leading advocate of a plan to draw a line westward to the Pacific to bisect the nation into equal halves, slave and free. He played a leading role in the Nashville Convention of 1850, organized in response to Northern efforts to ban slavery in the new Western territories. Davis was fully prepared to secede to prevent inroads on slavery. In 1853, Franklin Pierce appointed him secretary of war, and Davis transferred his nationalist spirit to the country at large. But when he returned to the Senate in 1857, Davis resumed his place at the head of the Southern resistance. He was a tall, gaunt man with sunken cheeks—like Lincoln himself. He had, unlike Lincoln, the dubious gift of self-certainty. As Varina had put it in her letter home, Davis had "a way of taking for granted that everyone agrees with him when he expresses an opinion."

Davis and Benjamin shared a passionate conviction about the rightness of the Southern cause, but in many ways belonged to different Souths. The one was a suave and epicurean product of the cosmopolitan culture of New Orleans, the other a Spartan and doctrinaire military leader—a fusion of South and West. Why did Benjamin issue a challenge to this grim warrior? He would have known that he was every bit as mismatched against Davis as Alexander Hamilton had been against Aaron Burr; but the code of honor demanded that he put his life at forfeit. Benjamin had never been so fully a Southerner—or never so committed to his life-long performance of the role of Southern gentleman—as he was at this moment. His story might well have ended as Hamilton's did. Fortunately, the moment Davis received the note, he said, "I will make this all right at once. I have been wholly wrong." This was one of the few recorded examples of a second thought in Davis's long career.

The Mississippi senator proceeded to apologize on the Senate floor, although only the two of them, and Bayard, knew of the proposed duel. Benjamin's show of courage, and Davis's of remorse, melted the ice between them.[30]

By the time of the contretemps with Davis the nation was hurtling inexorably toward civil war. The Democratic party itself was now divided down the middle. Stephen Douglas had foolishly imagined that he could bridge the abyss between slave and free with the doctrine of popular sovereignty. In late 1857 the Kansas territorial government had drawn up a pro-slavery and deeply undemocratic constitution—and then refused to submit it to a popular referendum, since free-soilers by this time outnumbered slave forces. Douglas could not swallow so patent a violation of popular sovereignty, and abruptly joined the Republicans in refusing to accept the document. In April 1860, Southern delegates walked out of the Democratic convention in Charleston that nominated Douglas for president. The following month, Benjamin denounced Douglas as a hypocrite in a long and, by his temperate standards, vitriolic Senate speech. Douglas had clung to his doctrine of popular sovereignty even after the Supreme Court had appeared to invalidate it by deciding in *Dred Scott* that slavery could not be forbidden in the territories. The North argued that the decision discredited the Court and did not have the force of law. The South regarded it as settled law. Douglas had promised to let his views be guided by the Court; but the Court had unexpectedly reached a decision that rendered his views untenable. He could neither embrace *Dred Scott* nor repudiate it.

Benjamin proceeded to hoist Douglas on his own petard, as he had Sumner; perhaps he had mastered this trick while cross-examining witnesses. The Louisiana senator read out excerpts from the famous Illinois senatorial debate of 1858 in which Douglas and Abraham Lincoln posed questions to one another. Lincoln had answered all of Douglas's questions un-equivocally, both acknowledging the right of slavery to persist in the South and affirming "the right of Congress to prohibit slavery in all the United States Territories" in direct defiance of *Dred Scott.* "It is impossible," Benjamin said, "however we may differ with the man, not to admire the perfect candor and frank-ness with which these answers were given."

Benjamin then turned to the meandering response Douglas gave to Lincoln. The senator from Illinois, hoping to preserve his appeal to anti-slavery voters, had insisted that a territorial legislature could prohibit slavery—"no matter what the deci-sion of the Supreme Court might be on that abstract question." Douglas had reduced the most consequential judicial decision of the century to a theoretical exercise. He was trying, perhaps jesuitically, to find a middle ground that would mollify both sides. Lincoln had cut out that ground from under him; Ben-jamin now proceeded to do so from the opposite direction. Having abandoned the pro-slavery position, Benjamin declared, Douglas "will be driven step by step, back and back, to the Black Republican camp. . . . Let him beware lest he get so far that return becomes impossible." (A "black Republican" was an arch-Republican—ergo, an abolitionist.) Until 1857, Benjamin observed in closing, more than a trifle disingenuously, he would have yielded to no man in his regard for Stephen Douglas. "It has been with reluctance and sorrow," he lamented, "that I have been obliged to pluck down my idol from his place on high."[31]

Southern Democrats were so delighted with Benjamin's evisceration of Douglas that they printed up his speech in pam-phlet form to serve as a campaign document for Kentucky sen-ator John C. Breckinridge, who would become the nominee of the breakaway Southern Democratic faction. Benjamin himself would sit out the election. He could never be granted a leader-ship role in a party dedicated to the preservation of an archaic way of life—even if he fully shared its principles. And unlike

Jefferson Davis, he had to work for a living. That is what he now left Washington to do.

In August 1860, Benjamin traveled to San Francisco, where he had been hired by English investors whose California silver mine, originally purchased prior to California's accession to the Union by Andres Castillero, a Mexican national, had been seized as American property. The litigation had gone on for years before it was ready to be heard in federal court. The investors then turned to the finest legal minds money could buy—Benjamin and Reverdy Johnson—to contest the legitimacy of the seizure. Benjamin summed up his client's case over six days in late October and early November. The San Francisco public and press treated the oration of this celebrated litigator as high entertainment; Benjamin's summation provoked thunderous applause.

The district court judges came down on his client's side. The investors, however, were foolish enough to appeal a portion of the decision to the Supreme Court, where the judgment was overturned in 1863, a time when Benjamin was scarcely available for legal work in Washington. The lawmaker sailed for home November 10. He would be paid $25,000—worth about $750,000 today—for his work.[32]

On November 7, 1860, the day after Lincoln was elected, Benjamin delivered a speech on American government at an Episcopal church in San Francisco. Carried away by his vision of national glory, as he often was when he contemplated the Western frontier, Benjamin rhapsodized over "the majestic march of our Union, which, like the great river upon whose banks I dwell, still pursues its resistless course into the unknown ocean that lies beyond." Yet events had reduced Benjamin's boosterism to hollow rhetoric. He warned his listeners that "the horrid sectional disputes, which now stun our ears with discordant din," would never be silenced unless the North accepted the intent of the Constitution as Southerners understood it.[33]

Events moved with dreadful speed. Congress reconvened

on December 3rd. On the 9th, Benjamin wrote to his New York friend Dr. Barlow, to whom he had once recommended a recipe for coffee. He described a meeting of Southern senators the day before at which he had cautioned against fantastic schemes to preserve the Union, and "implored them all to devote all their energies to devising means for rendering the separation peaceful if possible." He did not, however, see "how bloodshed is to be avoided," for "belief in the justice, wisdom and prudence of secession is blended with the keenest sense of wrong and outrage." This was the clear-headed and even-keeled counselor who was soon to play a calming role among the Confederate fire-eaters. All agreed that the Union had become unsustainable. The senators sent to their constituents a letter stating that, all efforts at compromise having been rejected by the Republicans, "we are satisfied the honor, safety and independence of the Southern people are to be found in a Southern Confederacy."

On New Year's Eve, Benjamin delivered the most storied speech of his life. South Carolina had already seceded; the others would soon do the same. Benjamin spoke not of slavery but of states' rights, the high principle on which the slave owners sought to peg their cause. With his characteristic flair for the ingenious conceit, he described the switch from the Articles of Confederation to the Constitution as an act of "secession," for the latter had been ratified without the approval of North Carolina or Rhode Island. He roamed over the debates of the Constitutional Convention, showing that the Framers had rejected all efforts to grant the federal government explicit powers to coerce the states. He dilated at length upon the Virginia and Kentucky Resolutions that had laid the foundation for the argument for "nullification." He quoted Emer de Vattel, the eighteenth-century legal theorist, to support his claim that foreign nations must acknowledge the sovereignty of seceded states. The South had done no more than assert its rights under the Constitution; and yet, said Benjamin, addressing the North, "you assert, and practice upon the assertion, that it is right to hold us up to the ban of mankind . . . as thieves, robbers, murderers, villains and criminals of the blackest dye, because we continue to own property that we owned at the time that we all signed the compact."

All this time, Benjamin stood by his desk rather than in the well of the Senate, so that his speech felt less like a formal oration than a personal statement. He kept one hand thrust in his pocket; with the other he fingered his watch chain. He spoke in the sonorous and modulated voice that his colleagues had come to know so well. Varina later wrote that "he held his audience spellbound for over an hour and so still were they that a whisper could have been heard." At last Benjamin reached the majestic climax without which no Southern speech could be accorded a place in the pantheon of oratory. He addressed himself, at the last, to his colleagues in the North:

> You may carry desolation in to our peaceful land; . . . you may, under the protection of your advancing armies, give protection to the furious fanatics who desire, and profess to desire, nothing more than to add all the horrors of a servile insurrection to the calamities of civil war; you may do all this—and more, if more there be—but you never can subjugate us; you never can convert the free sons of the soil into vassals, paying tribute to your power; and you never, never can degrade them to the level of an inferior and servile race. Never! Never![34]

As he intoned what appeared to be his final sentence, Benjamin released his watch chain in a gesture of finality and moved to sit. Then he rose up again for the final repeated cry of "Never!" The galleries, already raised to a fever pitch, burst into applause, shouts, huzzahs. The hubbub would not die down, and finally Senator James Mason of Virginia, presiding, ordered the sergeant-at-arms to clear the right-hand gallery.[35]

For years afterward, children in the South would recite portions of Benjamin's New Year's Eve speech, and above all the thundered "nevers." The speech secured Benjamin's place as one of the great Southern speakers of the era. "He was peerless as an orator," wrote Christian F. Eckloff, a Senate page who devoted a chapter to Benjamin in his memoirs. "To listen to him was like listening to music; he spoke with such ease, with such eloquence, and entirely without notes, save at times he might have a book or a single sheet from which he desired to speak. He engaged in all the important debates; and was a master in every maneuver of parliamentary art."[36] Senator George Vest of Missouri later remarked that, "though I have known greater leaders in legislation and political management than Judah P. Benjamin, I have never met his equal as an accomplished, well equipped and ready debater and legislator." Vest added that when he had asked Dennis Murphy, the Senate's veteran official reporter, whom he considered the "ablest" legislator he had known, the latter had replied without hesitation, "Judah P. Benjamin of Louisiana."[37]

In an alternate universe not defined by the issues of slavery and union, Benjamin would have been recalled as one of the great orators of the generation following Webster, Calhoun, and Clay. Had he steered clear of those issues, Benjamin would have come down to us as a gifted politician and one of the great litigators of his day. One can, in fact, find just such a trajectory in Benjamin's near-doppelgänger, Philip Phillips, a Jewish lawyer from Charleston born four years before Benjamin. Phillips, too, moved westward, to Mobile, where he was elected to the House the same year Benjamin joined the Senate. But Phillips was a moderate who privately opposed slavery; Stephen Douglas asked him to cobble together the language that would push Kansas-Nebraska through Congress. After one term, Phillips returned to private practice, but remained in Washington, where he befriended Jefferson Davis as well as future members of Abraham Lincoln's cabinet.

Phillips also opposed secession; when the war broke out, he remained in Washington, though he sided with the South. His career was almost destroyed by his wife, the notorious Eugenia Levy Phillips, who was arrested as a spy for the Confederacy, which indeed she was. Yet after the war the Phillipses were allowed to return to Washington, where Philip became a celebrated member of the Supreme Court bar.[38] Had Benjamin shared Phillips's convictions, he would have been neither lionized in the South nor hated in the North.

Southern states began following South Carolina into secession on January 5th. Louisiana voted to secede January 26th. Benjamin delivered his farewell speech to the chamber on February 4th. This time, melodramatically, he wore a pistol at his side. His closing words served as an elegiac text to be memorized and repeated in the South for decades to come:

> When, in after days, the story of the present shall be written; when history shall have passed her stern sentence on the erring men who have driven their unoffending brethren from the shelter of their common home . . . your children shall hear repeated the familiar tale . . . and they will glory in their lineage from men of spirit as generous and of patriotism as high hearted as ever illustrated or adorned the American Senate.[39]

Grown men wept—Benjamin himself not excepted. The senator from Louisiana had delivered the advance epitaph for the Lost Cause.

4

Richmond

In May 1861, the celebrated British journalist William Howard Russell paid a visit to the temporary Confederate government in Montgomery, Alabama. Having just come from Washington, Russell was startled to find the regime quartered in a modest brick building with pieces of paper stuck to the doorframe of each office proclaiming the cabinet department in question. The place was almost empty. Russell was first ushered into the office of President Jefferson Davis, whom he found elaborately hospitable but "rather reserved and drastic." Russell observed the fifty-one-year-old Confederate leader closely, noting a forehead covered with innumerable wrinkles, thin lips, high cheekbones and hollow jaws. One eye was filmed over, an effect of an ulceration that many found forbidding. (He was sometimes called "the Cyclops.") "The expression of his face is anxious," Russell wrote; "he has a very haggard, careworn and pain-drawn look." Yet, Russell added, "no trace of anything but the utmost confidence and the greatest decision could be detected in his conversation."

Russell met briefly with Secretary of War LeRoy Walker, and then was directed to the office of Judah Benjamin. As the attorney general of a state that had no judicial system, Benjamin was the least significant member of the cabinet, but he had already become the man to see for journalists and other important visitors. Russell made the obligatory references to Benjamin's "most decidedly Jewish features," including among them, as others did not, "the brightest large black eyes, one of which is somewhat diverse from the other." Russell was delighted by Benjamin's "brisk, lively, agreeable manner, combined with much vivacity of speech and quickness of utterance." The two men plunged without ceremony into a discussion of England's posture toward the Confederacy. "Mr. Benjamin did not appear afraid of anything," Russell observed, "but his confidence respecting Great Britain was based a good deal, no doubt, on his firm faith in cotton, and in England's utter subjection to her cotton interest and manufactures." Benjamin was quite certain that England would soon recognize the Confederacy despite its "coyness about acknowledging a slave power."[1]

Davis and Benjamin shared an invincible faith in the prospects of the infant Confederacy, though for quite different reasons. Davis was a holy warrior to whom doubt was foreign, while Benjamin was an advocate and a promoter who had learned to persuade others, and no doubt himself, of the merits of whatever cause he had undertaken. Benjamin would spend the ensuing four years hypnotizing visitors and doubters in the Confederate ranks with his dazzling certainties. Yet he may never have been quite so sure of the outcome as he led others to believe he was; Benjamin was a watchful, calculating man who loved to gamble but did not lose track of the odds against him.

Benjamin had left Washington for New Orleans immediately after delivering his farewell oration. Back home, he delivered an address before a crowd of twenty thousand gathered to commemorate George Washington's birthday. Benjamin acknowledged that the North would not accept secession without a fight and reassured his listeners of the cleansing virtues of violence: "The fire sweeps over the stubble and the charred and blackened surface of the field attests its ravage. Yet a little while and the spring rains descend."[2] With just such lulling metaphors did the South rock itself to sleep in the months before the Civil War broke out.

Benjamin did not yet know what role, if any, he would have in the government of the South. A convention of Southern states meeting in Montgomery had asked Jefferson Davis to serve as president. Davis, who had longed for the post of military commander, very reluctantly accepted a job for which he was far less well suited, and traveled to Montgomery along with Varina to take up his responsibilities. Davis assembled a cabinet whose sole distinguishing feature was geographical inclusivity; the skepticism of the Southern states about any form of central administration must have convinced him of the need to give each an obvious stake in the new government. From Louisiana he chose Benjamin, still largely a stranger to him, to serve in the essentially ceremonial post of attorney general. Davis would later write that he had selected the Louisiana senator for "the lucidity of his intellect, his systematic habits and capacity for labor."[3] He would not be disappointed in any of those respects.

Southerners had long played an outsized role at West Point and in the ranks of senior officers; Davis and his chief advisers, including LeRoy Walker, the secretary of war, had convinced themselves that, despite its disadvantage in sheer numbers, the Confederacy's martial superiority would quickly manifest itself on the battlefield. The Lincoln administration would see the folly of further hostilities and leave the South to constitute itself as a new nation. Benjamin shared their confidence in the final outcome, though not in its simplicity or speed; to that extent one may say that he was a realist among dreamers. At the first Cabinet meeting in Montgomery, according to an account from Walker, "there was only one man there who had any sense and that man was Benjamin. Mr. Benjamin proposed that the government purchase as much cotton as it could hold, at least 100,000 bales, and ship it at once to England."[4] (A bale of cotton weighed 500 pounds.) The proceeds would be used to buy guns and ammunition, which the South had very little industrial capacity to produce, with the remainder available for credit, which the South could hardly count on. The proposal was voted down as unnecessary and perhaps even defeatist. Walker would come to rue his own over-confidence, and that of his colleagues.

Hostilities did not begin until the middle of April, when Confederate forces under General P. G. T. Beauregard fired on federal troops in Fort Sumter, in the harbor of Charleston, and seized the facility. President Lincoln responded by issuing a call for 75,000 volunteers. The Southern states that had remained on the sidelines, including Virginia and North Carolina, then voted to secede. At that point the Confederate government could leave Montgomery, hot and fly-ridden and cramped, for Richmond, the gracious state capital laid out by Thomas Jefferson barely a hundred miles from Washington. In June, while an interval of peace persisted, during which both sides mustered their forces, the government decamped.

Benjamin, the Davises, and much of the Cabinet took rooms at the Spotswood Hotel at the corner of Main and Eighth Street. The hotel was located immediately below the Capitol building, Jefferson's homage to classical republicanism, and the broad park in which it sat. The Customs House, across the street from the Capitol, served as the temporary offices of government. For the next four months or so, until both Benjamin and the Davises moved out to permanent quarters, the hallways and the dining room of the Spotswood functioned as the nerve center of the Confederacy.

On July 21, Union General Irvin McDowell attempted to outflank the Confederate army under General Beauregard. The two forces met at Bull Run, near Manassas Junction in Virginia. During the course of the battle Beauregard's forces were reinforced by troops serving under Generals Thomas "Stonewall" Jackson and Joe Johnston, as well as Jeb Stuart and Jubal Early—soon to become the most celebrated military commanders in the South. The Union forces broke and fled in retreat. In the first battle of the Civil War, the South had won a shattering victory.

Like an old war horse hearing the bugle call, Jefferson Davis had bolted from Richmond for the battlefield; he would always be far more comfortable as the Confederacy's commanding general than as president, though the South had many more capable generals than it did civilian administrators. As soon as the outcome was clear, he sent a cable to Varina announcing victory. Benjamin, who had joined his cabinet colleagues at the War Department, left for the Spotswood, where he knew that he would find Varina. She read him the cable, which Benjamin promptly committed to memory. He then raced back to the War Department, by then crowded with reporters and clerks and the wives of officials, called for silence and, "his eyes on fire," as one subaltern recorded, recited the message from Davis: "We have gained a glorious but dear-bought victory. Night closed upon the enemy in full flight and closely pursued." There were shouts of joy; as in all battles before and after this one, "glorious" had sunk in long before "dear-bought."[5]

Nor was Davis's message entirely accurate, for McDowell's forces had not been "closely pursued"; quite the opposite. Inexperienced Union soldiers had flung away their weapons on a desperate flight back to Washington. Neither Beauregard nor Johnston pressed their advantage; they took several hundred prisoners, but lost the precious opportunity to inflict devastating losses and approach the nation's capital. As it was, 460 Union soldiers, and 387 from the Confederate side, were killed—an unimaginable toll for the day, though of course soon to be eclipsed by far bloodier battles. Recriminations over the failure to take the offensive began immediately, and focused less on the battlefield generals than on Secretary Walker, widely regarded as a mediocrity appointed only in order to represent Alabama in the Cabinet. Davis pressured him to resign. He did so on September 14, at which point Davis appointed Judah Benjamin as acting secretary.

While we can hardly be surprised that Davis would have chosen a supremely talented lawyer as his attorney general, the decision to make that drawing-room dandy, who barely knew how to mount a horse or heft a rifle, the secretary of war, and thus to take direct command over the icons of Southern manhood—Beauregard, Johnston, Jackson, Robert E. Lee—was extraordinary. No doubt the likeliest explanation is that Davis "considered himself the most competent Secretary of War in the Confederacy," as the modern Benjamin biographer Eli Evans writes, and thus needed "a dependable administrator to carry out his every order down to the last detail."[6] What's more, he needed someone who would not waver under public obloquy, and who would not sacrifice the good of the Confederacy to his own interests. Perhaps Davis also recognized that in the dawning era of industrial warfare, organizational skills mattered as much as martial ones. By this time he had spent enough time working closely with Benjamin that he understood his distinctive virtues; more important, he had come to trust his former Senate colleague.

At the heart of the Confederate government was the relationship between these two very unlike men. One could hardly call it equal, for Davis was the prince and Benjamin his senior courtier. It was Benjamin who had to be thinking at all times how he could serve and support Davis; yet by doing just this so very well, Benjamin made himself indispensable, as the most gifted courtiers do. "No shade of emotion in another escaped Mr. Benjamin," Varina Davis later wrote; "he seemed to have a kind of electric sympathy with every mind with which he came into contact."[7] Others were not so deeply struck by this empathic gift, but Varina saw Benjamin's relationship with Davis as no one else did. She described her husband as "abnormally sensitive to disapprobation; even a child's disapproval discomposed him."[8] He lived at an almost unbearable pitch of inner tension. Varina wrote that her husband typically "came home fasting a mere mass of throbbing nerves, and perfectly exhausted; but Mr. Benjamin was always fresh and buoyant." Benjamin had endured slights and humiliation from his earliest days; he had long since learned to keep the perpetual half-smile fixed to his face and return to work.

In an administration as skeletal as the Confederacy, Benjamin's matchless capacity for hard work made him a precious—and rare—commodity. "He accomplishes more business in one hour than most men can accomplish in a day," a correspondent for the Richmond *Courier* wrote after a visit in October. "Mr. Benjamin is one of the most extraordinary men in America, and is almost indispensable to the Confederacy." The reporter added that "no public man has a larger share of the confidence of the President."[9] Davis himself lacked the gift of delegation, and wished to be everywhere at once. In this he found a perfect partner in Benjamin. "Sometimes," Varina wrote, "with half an hour's recess he remained with the Executive from 10 in the morning until nine at night, and together they traversed all the difficulties which encompassed our beleaguered land."[10] In a letter written to a friend after the war, Benjamin acknowledged what never would have escaped his lips at the time, that he had written Davis's messages to Congress, since Davis had been too busy to do so himself.[11]

In the war's initial campaigns, at Bull Run and then at Ball's

Bluff three months later, the South had carried the day through a combination of bravado and the incompetence of Union commanders. Neither could be counted on in the long run. Industrial capacity and the management of logistics would become ever more important; but the slave system, with its culture of white leisure, had rendered the Southern economy almost wholly agrarian. Whatever might become possible in the future, should the war prove protracted, at first the South had to look abroad for almost everything. By the summer of 1861 the Union Navy had clamped a blockade on all major Southern ports, severely limiting both exports and imports. The South had, at least initially, enough men; but not enough weapons, powder, clothing, tents.

As soon as he took over the War Department, Benjamin began fielding dispatches from his generals clamoring for equipment. In late September, General Albert Sidney Johnston, commander of Western forces, wrote from Nashville pleading for muskets. Benjamin responded that a shipment of arms from England had just arrived but included only 1,800 Enfield rifles, of which he had had to send a thousand to the governor of Georgia. Confederate stores contained only 2,500 rifles, of which, Benjamin said, "I have ordered 1000 sent to you, leaving us but 1500 for arming several regiments camped here, and who have been awaiting their arms for several months."[12] Years would pass before the Tredegar Iron Works in Richmond could turn out a steady supply of guns and cannon. For its small arms in the meantime, the South depended on a supply route that ran from Europe to the West Indies, and then, by means of blockade-running ships, to Southern ports. Agents for the Union stationed in Europe often managed to outbid Confederate buyers for the scarce supply.

The relationship between the war secretary and the generals was unavoidably conflictual, for they desperately needed what he could not give. Although Albert Sidney Johnston always wrote respectfully to Benjamin, the same could not be said for many of his colleagues; and Benjamin was quick to reciprocate. When General Joseph Johnston, commander of the Confederate Army of the Potomac, implored Benjamin to send up ammunition and men, the secretary harshly retorted, "We have not a single return from your army of the quantity of ammunition, artillery, means of transportation, or sick in camp or in hospital, to enable us to form a judgment of what your necessities may be."[13] Johnston was a military professional, but neither he nor many other senior commanders took seriously the need to inform Richmond of the state of affairs inside their camps. Benjamin, who after decades defending America's largest corporations understood very well how modern institutions worked, harped again and again on the need for accurate record-keeping.

The political culture of a nation founded on the principle of states' rights made Benjamin's work yet harder, for governors regarded themselves as sovereign rulers, and balked at whatever demands from Richmond they found unjust. Benjamin felt that he had to direct 1,000 muskets to Georgia governor Joseph E. Brown even when his own generals had to curtail operations for lack of armed men. In late September, Benjamin received a series of increasingly strident letters from North Carolina governor Henry T. Clark. "We have sent to Virginia 13,500 stand of arms," Clark wrote in one, "and now we are out of arms, and our soil invaded, and you refuse our request to send us back some of our own armed regiments to defend us." Benjamin instantly wrote back to explain that His Excellency was "strangely misinformed," for North Carolina had been given more arms than it could use. The truth was that no one had enough.

As fall turned into winter, the letters from the battlefield became increasingly painful to read. In mid-November, A. W. G. Davis, a local commander in the mountains of what is now

West Virginia, wrote Benjamin that he had waited until his clerks retired for the night to write him a personal letter. "This army is utterly demoralized," he wrote, "or if this term is too strong, it is the most disquieted collection of men I have ever known brought together." The men demanded to be taken down to the plains for the winter. Few Southern troops had been able to build winter quarters; many slept beneath tents. Nevertheless, Davis had compelled his men to remain in the increasingly frigid heights lest the far larger Union force surrounding them retake the territory they had abandoned—and more men die to retake it than would have perished from the elements. "I am now not acceptable to the army," the officer wrote despondently.[14]

Although Benjamin wrote regularly to his commanders in the field in order to direct troop movements, he would not have done so without first learning the wishes of Jefferson Davis. Because Benjamin always cited Davis as the source of any controversial directive, it's hard to know just how much latitude he had. The two consulted constantly, and so functioned as one joint mind. Nevertheless, knowing that he always had the president's support, Benjamin was prepared to forcefully impose his will.

In early November, Benjamin received a series of dispatches documenting the burning of railway bridges across eastern Tennessee, known to be a hotbed of Union sentiment. Absent forceful action, he was told, Southern lines would soon be cut in two. Benjamin ordered troops from Memphis and Pensacola to put down the uprising, which soon collapsed. Colonel W. B. Wood, the local Confederate commander, asked Benjamin what he should do with the rebels. He did not trust the civilian courts. "It is a mere farce to arrest them and turn them over to the courts," Wood wrote. "Instead of having the effect of intimidation it really gives encouragement and only emboldens them in their traitorous conduct."[15] The secretary cabled back to say that those who had not set fire to the bridges should be held as prisoners of war, while those alleged to have done so should be "tried summarily by drum-head court-martial, and, if found guilty, executed on the spot by hanging." Benjamin added that "It would be well to leave their bodies hanging in the vicinity of the burned bridges."[16]

The order was so harsh, even by the standards of military justice, that a senior officer on the spot cabled back asking for the president's express approval. Benjamin took the responsibility on himself. "The law does not require any approval by the President," he wrote back, "but he entirely approves my order to hang every bridge-burner you can catch and convict."[17] Andrew Johnson, a Tennessee senator and Unionist, would later declare that "the blood of these men, like Abel, cried aloud from the ground against the author of their death, and for succor to their wives and little ones."[18] Americans in an earlier age had recoiled from summary executions: When word reached Washington in 1817 that Andrew Jackson had tried and hanged two British spies in Florida, the House had spent twenty-seven days debating a resolution of censure (ultimately passed in the Senate, but not in the House). But far less seemed to be at stake in that raid against rebellious Indian tribes; the Tennessee insurgency threatened the integrity of the Confederacy. And the violence of feeling on both sides made men murderous. When Union forces took New Orleans in April 1862, residents tore down an American flag from the Mint. General Ben Butler found a man with a shred of bunting in his buttonhole—and had him court-martialed and summarily hanged from a window of the Mint.

Civilian life remained gracious in the first years of the war; and Richmond was very much to Judah Benjamin's taste. The city sloped up from the James River, always teeming with ships, like the harbors in Charleston and New Orleans. The tobacco industry that once supported Richmond had largely given way to the production of iron and flour; the northern bank of the James was crowded with flour mills and warehouses. Main Street, the city's chief commercial thoroughfare, was lined with three-story row houses whose ground floors were occupied by shops, as well as by large banks and hotels. From there the city rose steeply to the north; at the brow of the hill stood the Capitol, the highest point save the spires of the surrounding churches— St. Paul's Episcopal and St. Peter's, the Catholic church. Around the corner from the Capitol, at Odd Fellows Hall, stood the city's chief slave market. Richmond's single greatest source of wealth was the sale of slaves who were then sent southward and westward, to plantation centers like New Orleans.

At the outset of the war, Richmond had a population of 39,000, of whom a quarter to a third were slaves—far smaller than New Orleans or Washington, but large enough to support a sizeable class of lawyers, doctors, and businessmen. What's more, like Charleston and New Orleans, Richmond had what passed in America for ancient roots, and aristocratic families whose wealth came from the land. Richmond's nobility—the FFV, or "First Families of Virginia"—comported itself with a formality that would have met the approval of Regency England. As George Cary Eggleston, himself an FFV, put it, "To come from a good family is a patent of nobility, and there is no other way whatever by which any man or woman can find a passage into the charmed circle of Virginia's peerage."[19]

Benjamin had, of course, a gift for gliding into such charmed circles. In any case, the war created a new social hierarchy in which he occupied the uppermost tier. Thomas Cooper De Leon, a Southern Jewish journalist and a Confederate soldier during the war, observed that "there was no circle, official or otherwise, that missed his soft, purring presence, or had not regretted so doing. . . . He moved into or through the most elegant or the simplest assemblage on natural rubber tires and well-oiled bearings."[20] Even a fellow Jew, it turns out, could be faintly repelled by Benjamin's smooth and obliging manner.

In October 1861, the Davises left the Spotswood for the former home of the Brockenbrough family, a pillared eighteenth-century mansion on a quiet square just north of the Capitol. Renamed the Confederate White House, it served as a passable imitation of the original. Across Clay Street were the fine brick homes occupied by Vice President Alexander Stephens and Senator James Chesnut and his wife Mary, who would later write a famous memoir of the war years. Benjamin certainly had the wherewithal to rent one of Richmond's great homes and stay close to Davis's orbit. He chose instead to take a plain two-story house on Main Street, about a mile south and west of the White House. Benjamin had never lavished much care on himself. When he was not trying to seduce Natalie with opulence he lived modestly, whether in New Orleans, Washington, or Richmond. Benjamin moved to the so-called Davenport House, at 9 West Main, with Duncan Kenner, a Louisiana congressman and old friend, and his young brother-in-law, Jules St. Martin.

Benjamin treated Jules almost as a stand-in for Natalie; Jules had all of his sister's languid charm with none of her complacency or self-absorption. The older man doted on his charge. Varina would later write,

> When he first spoke of Mr. Saint Martin, whom we did not at the time know at all, I thought he must be a very charming boy of twelve or fifteen years old; and when the refined, accomplished young gentleman of perhaps thirty years old made his bow to me in Washington, I found difficulty in believing this was the "Jules, dear little fellow, who will be lonesome if I do not go home," with whose name all Mr. Benjamin's particular friends were intimate.[21]

Varina described Benjamin saving choice morsels off his plate to bring home for his brother-in-law. At times she almost seems to be hinting at an excess of devotion, whether out of jealousy—for Varina seemed to love this man who intuited the feelings of all others—or out of an uneasy sense that his devotion to Jules was unmanly. She records a moment when Jules, embarrassed by Benjamin's "caressing words," objects to being treated like a child, to which the older man responds, "No man ever loved his child any better, but love like ours must be founded on respect, at least mine is such for you." We can't help wondering, not so much whether Benjamin had a sexual relationship with Jules, which we cannot know, but whether his infatuation was a means to indulge an otherwise repressed love of men, and not simply the absence of family. One can hardly doubt the depth of the devotion: Benjamin seemed deathly afraid of seeing Jules go off to war, and ensured that this would not happen by finding him a clerical job in the War Department.

Benjamin's intellectual clarity and tireless work habits served him well as an administrator; but there was little he, or anyone, could do about the clash of ambitions among the South's leading generals, or about the immense frustrations they felt when their plans ran into the limits of available men and matériel. By the fall of 1861, the generals were barely staying in harness. At times Davis scarcely held his own temper in check; but more often he responded emolliently, addressing his anguished interlocutor as "my dear general." The act of writing a letter seemed to put Davis in an expansive mood, and his missives tended to be long and decorated with literary allusions. Benjamin, the great orator, was all business; he was able to dispense with his massive correspondence file only by chiseling away all excess sentiment. One note, to General Ben McCullouch in Springfield, Arkansas, read in its entirely, "I cannot understand why you withdrew your troops instead of pursuing the enemy when his leaders were quarreling and his army separated into parts under different commanders. Send an explanation."[22] He understood that these men, some of them objects of veneration across the South, would not take kindly to curt instructions from a civilian—and a Jew, to boot. He enjoyed the protection of President Davis—and they knew he did. But Benjamin could not have written as he did without tremendous confidence in his own judgment: his entire career had demonstrated the superiority of his own abilities. He did not need this job; and he would do nothing that he felt would damage the war effort in the name of keeping it.

In October, Benjamin rebuked Beauregard, the hero of Bull Run, for trying to recruit a rocket battery from the troops in Richmond without notifying the War Department. Even worse, for Beauregard, was Benjamin's magnanimous declaration that he would not punish the general's "defect of judgment" since the latter had not intended to do wrong. Rather than respond to a man he regarded as a pettifogging clerk, Beauregard sent off a fabulously intemperate letter to Davis pointing out Benjamin's "unusual and offensive style" and asking the president to choose between "your general, who has simply done what was *essential* to provide the men to handle the rockets as soon as ready for use" and "that functionary at his desk," ready to "write lectures on law while the enemy is mustering on our front."

That wasn't all. Beauregard wrote another letter demanding to be treated as, in effect, co-commander, with Joe Johnston, of a single army—or to be relieved of his "false position." This was only the first of what would become innumerable threats to resign by Confederate generals fired with an exalted sense of honor. Perhaps Davis should have responded; but it was Benjamin who did so. "I beg to say in all kindness," he wrote, with that show of politesse that had rankled men far more temperate than General Beauregard, "that it is not your position that is false but your idea of the organization of the Army. . . . you are second in command of the *whole* army of the Potomac, and not *first* in command of *half* the army." Benjamin continued in the vein of bravura logic-chopping that had served him so well in the courtroom, concluding that President Davis himself had "found the same error as to the organization of the army which you seem to entertain . . . generally prevalent."

Once again Beauregard responded with a furious missive to Davis, demanding that the latter "shield me from these ill-timed, unaccountable annoyances." Davis had responded chaffingly to the first letter, proposing that the general "dismiss this small matter from your mind" in order to focus on "the hostile masses before you." Now he dropped the jocund tone, which in any case was alien to him. "I do not feel competent to instruct Mr. Benjamin in the matter of style," he told Beauregard; "there are few whom the public would believe fit, probably, for the task." Surely, he said, the general could not regard himself or his army as "outside the limits of the law." In any case, Davis wrote forbiddingly, "It is my duty to see that the laws are faithfully executed and I cannot recognize the pretension of anyone that the restraint is narrow for him." Davis had, in fact, chosen between his general and his secretary of war, but not the way Beauregard had envisioned.[23]

Benjamin survived each of these encounters thanks to Davis's unflinching support, which he had earned by knowing the latter's will and carrying it out no matter the consequences. "Functionary" though he was, Benjamin was prepared to be bloody-minded when necessary.

Here as elsewhere, Benjamin was carrying out Davis's will. Davis was the Confederacy's president and commander-in-chief; ultimate responsibility for the war campaign rested with him. But in a state born in rebellion and able to establish itself only through war, the generals in the field could not bring themselves to accept the president's military supremacy. They could not defy so universally revered a figure, but when Davis's orders came through his secretary of war, they could, and did, resist. In January 1862, Stonewall Jackson had earned his reputation, and his nickname, rampaging through West Virginia and reclaiming large amounts of territory for the Confederacy. Toward the end of the month, Jackson returned to fortified areas, leaving a division in the "exposed and cheerless village" of Romney. After receiving alarming reports both of Union movements in the area and of the extreme vulnerability of the Confederate position, Benjamin ordered Jackson to pull his men back to safety. Jackson complied, but added a poisonous note, which he repeated to anyone who cared to listen: "With such interference in my command I cannot expect to be of much service in the field." Jackson asked to be returned to his professorship at Virginia Military Institute. Failing that, he wrote, "I respectfully request that the President accept my resignation from the Army."

The generals were quite sure that Stonewall Jackson mattered more to the Confederacy than Judah Benjamin. Jackson's friends, including General Joe Johnston and Virginia governor John Letcher, wrote him supporting his sense of grievance and heaping blame on the secretary of war. Johnston wrote to Benjamin saying that he had caused "great consternation and an approach to demoralization" by interfering in military prerogative. When Benjamin declined to respond, the general repeated the same allegations to Davis—who in fact believed that Jackson had spread out his forces too thinly, and had instructed his secretary of war to issue the order to Jackson. The president, again, backed up his secretary against his senior officers in the field.[24]

Having failed in their frontal assault, Benjamin's enemies now mounted a whispering campaign against him. Asked at a dinner party whether the Confederacy could win with Benjamin in his current position, General Johnston answered in the negative, a rebuke that was sure to make its way rapidly around town. John B. Jones, a clerk in the War Department and a rabid anti-Semite, preserved in his diary a running tally of poisonous tales spread about his boss. In late October he reported that Benjamin was said to have held on to memberships in the leading clubs of New York and Boston. (Benjamin had in fact remained a member of New York's Union Club, which refused to expel him and other Confederate officials, leading to the formation of the rival Union League Club.) In December he blamed Benjamin for releasing prisoners, who it was said had then spread disinformation to Confederate generals, leading to the death of troops. Benjamin was also said to have granted passports to Northerners who wished to return home—and thus, it was alleged, report on conditions in the South.[25]

Loyalties are everything in wartime, and Benjamin's Jewishness gave all the license needed to the sentiment that he was "not one of us." As early as the Montgomery convention in February 1861, Thomas R. R. Cobb, younger brother of Georgia's political leader Howell Cobb, wrote, "A grander rascal than this Jew Benjamin does not exist in the Confederacy, and I am not particular in concealing my opinion of him." In the mind of the younger Cobb, the secretary of war was not only not a Christian; he was not a man. In a letter to his wife in January 1862, he revived old rumors: "Speaking of Jews, this little contemptible prosecutor of Howells and mine, Benjamin, Secretary of War, is an eunuch. The poor fool to try and hide it, married." Then his wife had left for Paris, where she took lovers, Cobb explained. "This is the 'on-dit' of the City." That, and more, was the talk of the town.[26] In her war diary, Mary Chesnut wrote in February 1862 that while her husband considered Benjamin "the very cleverest man we had in the Senate. . . . The mob only calls him Mr. Davis' pet Jew, a King Street Jew, cheap, very cheap, &c&c."[27] Henry Foote, a member of the Confederate Congress, thought of Benjamin as "Davis' dapper little attaché."[28]

Benjamin had struggled all his life to free himself of his Jewish identity, to be regarded only as a lawyer, an agriculturalist, a statesman, a deal-maker and a member in the highest possible standing of Southern society. He had succeeded to a degree scarcely imaginable. Yet now, at the very pinnacle, many of the people around him, and in the broader public, saw him as Jefferson Davis's court Jew, a figure of legend, a rank outsider who had nefariously wormed his way into the heart of power. Richmond's chief newspaper, the *Examiner*, never tired of attacks against Benjamin personally and the city's Jews in general, whom the paper regarded as a fifth column. The Jews, the editors wrote in 1862, "have flocked here as vultures and birds of passage," avoiding conscription by professing foreign allegiance while Christian boys rode to the slaughter. The Confederate Congress rang with denunciations of Benjamin and of Jews. The most virulent of the members, Henry Foote of Mississippi, was obsessed with Benjamin, declaring that he would never permit the South to establish a Supreme Court "so long as Judah P. Benjamin shall continue to pollute the ears of majesty Davis with his insidious counsels."[29] (Foote would later turn on Davis as well.)

Benjamin knew that it was part of his job to accept blame for the painful decisions the Confederate leader had to make. Did he have to endure yet more abuse for the accident of his Jewish birth? We can't help but wonder what he thought as he gazed around the Cabinet, or met with his generals. In the absence of evidence, it is the province of literature rather than biography to pose such questions; and in *John Brown's Body*, his epic poem on the Civil War, Stephen Vincent Benét did just that by projecting himself into Benjamin's mind. The poem was written in 1928, more than sixty years after the end of the war, but it's likely that Benét had read Pierce Butler's biography. He offers a version of Benjamin that we can fix in our mind's eye:

> Judah P. Benjamin, the dapper Jew,
> Seal-sleek, black-eyed, lawyer and epicure,
> Able, well-hated, face alive with life,
> Looked round the council-chamber with the slight
> Perpetual smile he held before himself
> Continually like a silk-ribbed fan.
> Behind the fan, his quick, shrewd, fluid mind
> Weighed Gentiles in an old balance. . . .
>
> I hide myself behind a smiling fan.
> They hide themselves behind a Gentile mask
> And if they fall, they will be lifted up,
> Being the people, but if I once fall
> I fall forever, like the rejected stone.[30]

Benjamin always strove to give the impression that he was not striving to give an impression. But he saw through the "Gentile mask" of collegiality; he knew very well that others did not regard him as one of them. Yet he could be accepted in this Christian tribe only if he behaved *as if* he belonged, and as if they believed he did. He had to flawlessly imitate nonchalance—thus the ingratiating smile and the "silk-ribbed fan," with its suggestion of hiding in plain sight. That fan, of course, also carries the suggestion of femininity. Did *they* see that he bore the fan before him? Certainly they saw the "simpering" smile. They knew as well—and Benjamin knew that they knew—that as Southerners they could melt back into their world should their great gamble fail; he would not be permitted to do so.

The South endured no losses during Benjamin's first few months as secretary of war. Then it had several in quick succession. Confederate troops had fortified Roanoke Island off North Carolina in order to block the route inland both to that state and to southern Virginia. In mid-January the island's commander, General Henry Wise, a former Virginia senator and one of the most prominent men in the state, came to Richmond to implore Benjamin to quickly reinforce the 2,000 men on the island, threatened by a combined land and sea force under Union general Ambrose Burnside. Benjamin enraged Wise by putting him off with vague promises. Benjamin knew, as Wise did not, that the South had no cannons, no powder, and no men to spare. Burnside turned out to have 13,000 men under his command and managed to overwhelm the island's defenses, continuing on to take a series of lightly guarded North Carolina cities and towns.

After the war Benjamin wrote to Colonel Charles Marshall, Robert E. Lee's aide-de-camp, explaining, as he could not have done at the time, the underlying reasons for the fiasco:

> I consulted the President whether it was best for the country that I should submit to unmerited censure or reveal to a Congressional Committee our poverty and my utter inability to supply the requisitions of General Wise, and thus run the risk that the fact should become known to some of the spies of the enemy, of whose activity we were well assured. It was thought best for the public service that I should suffer the blame in silence and a report of censure on me was accordingly made by the Committee of Congress.[31]

Rarely has the idea of Jew as scapegoat been so perfectly illustrated. Benjamin seems almost vain of the suffering he had agreed to endure for a higher cause.

The fall of Roanoke Island was bitter enough; but among the dead was General Wise's twenty-eight-year-old son Jennings, who had grown up in Richmond, became the precocious editor of the Richmond *Enquirer*, and served as commander of the local militia, the Richmond Blues. Jennings was adored; the city's most prominent citizens attended his funeral at St. James Episcopal. Benjamin had already run afoul of the Confederacy's most admired generals; now the city blamed him for the death of its favorite son. Davis would have to sack him. But the president could not live without him; he had come to rely on Benjamin too deeply.

Davis made a remarkable decision: he asked Secretary of State Robert Hunter—in whom, to be sure, he had very little confidence—to step down, and appointed Benjamin in his stead. Varina Davis later wrote that "the President promoted him to the State Department with an aggrieved sense of injustice done to the man who had now become his friend and right hand."[32] Few in Richmond shared that sense of grievance. In her memoir of the war years, Sallie Brock Putnam, a grande dame of the town, wrote that, although Benjamin was deemed "culpable" for the loss of Roanoke and the death of Jennings Wise, "we had the mortification to behold his promotion to a position of higher grade." Benjamin, she writes, was "ever afterwards unpopular in the Confederacy, and particularly in Virginia."[33]

Judah Benjamin had always known that the South would have to wade through blood in order to win its independence; but the ladies and gentlemen of Richmond had not known that, and the cavaliers who ran the Confederacy had denied it. It took almost a year after Fort Sumter for the full reality of the war to sink in.

In May 1862, the Union ironclad known as the *Monitor* advanced up the James River toward Richmond with a detachment of gunboats. The South had earlier been forced to scuttle its own ironclad, the *Merrimack*, rather than let it fall into the hands of the enemy, and Richmond now lay exposed. Soldiers as well as slaves furiously dug trenches and built fortifications. A mood of panic gripped the city. Jefferson Davis told Varina to leave with the children for North Carolina. Many of the city's women and children followed suit. Troops under General Robert E. Lee, who had spent the previous months fortifying

Savannah against naval attack, crossed the James River a few miles south of Richmond to engage vastly larger Union forces at Drewry's Bluff. Jefferson Davis and his cabinet, including Judah Benjamin, watched from the heights across the river until General Lee ordered them to leave lest they be mowed down by Union gunfire.

The Battle of Seven Days, as it came to be called, ended when the Union general George B. McClellan was forced to withdraw his troops. The engagement secured Lee's reputation as a master tactician. Yet it had been a dreadful slaughter. In the aftermath, McClellan described a vista of fallen Confederate soldiers, with "enough of them alive and moving to give the field a singular crawling effect."[34] The 20,000 Confederate dead and wounded were carried back into town, where they clogged the streets and overwhelmed the Hollywood Cemetery and the Chimborazo Hospital, both located on the hills above the city. McClellan lost 16,000 men. In addition, more than 5,000 Union prisoners were jammed into a facility on Belle Isle in the middle of the James, where they had been virtually abandoned to starve, to freeze, and to fall prey to infectious disease.

Richmond was now fully devoted to the business of war. The women of the first families volunteered to minister to wounded soldiers; homes and hotels were converted into impromptu clinics. Thousands of slaves had been temporarily conscripted from plantations to man the industrial sites pumping out weapons and clothing and flour. Smoke poured morning and night from the five great chimneys of the Tredegar Iron Works along the banks of the James River.[35] The population of the city had grown to over 100,000. Thousands of billeted soldiers in tents occupied the parks and the open spaces; the tromp-tromp-tromp of their drilling became the background noise to daily life. With them had come grifters and prostitutes and cheap hotels; a whorehouse set up shop across the street from the YMCA in the center of Richmond. Gambling halls proliferated. It was said that the secretary of state could sometimes be seen playing faro late into the night. Once, according to rumor, he had to slip out a back window to avoid a police raid—though the story can hardly be taken at face value, since it was spread by the Mississippi senator Henry Foote, who loathed Benjamin.[36]

Wartime Richmond was fearful, angry, suspicious. The very word "Yankee" became a term of abuse. Yankee spies were thought—not wrongly—to be everywhere. On March 1, 1862, Davis declared martial law in the city. The city's "provost marshal," Brigadier General John H. Winder, who also oversaw the growing prison system, had brought in a squad of detectives from Baltimore, where he had previously served. These street-hardened officers, widely derided as Northern "plug-uglies," were authorized to stop citizens on the street and demand identification. No one, not even the old guard, was immune from the constant demands for proof of identity, which infuriated the citizenry. Nor could citizens leave the city without a "passport" issued by the State Department—that is, by Benjamin. Winder bore the brunt of Richmond's hatred, but since he reported to Benjamin, the latter was also blamed for the crackdown.

Thanks to the Northern blockade, Richmond was also increasingly hungry. Varina Davis recorded the skyrocketing prices of all staples in November 1862, as currency inflated and supply diminished: coffee at $4 a pound, tea at $18 to $20 a pound, butter at $2 a pound—all two or four times what they had been in July.[37] The rich tightened their belts and felt proud of their sacrifice, while the poor feared starvation. On April 26, 1863, a butcher's assistant named Minerva Meredith harangued a growing crowd of hungry, desperate woman. Soon they were marching to the shops on Main Street, chanting "Bread, bread!" like the mobs of the French Revolution. The army of women smashed shop windows and plundered the goods inside. They were stopped only when Jefferson Davis rode into their midst. "I will give you five minutes to disperse," he said. "Otherwise you will be fired on." No one doubted that Davis was a man of his word. The women sullenly drifted away, clutching their war booty.[38]

Some of the Confederate leaders were going to pieces under the unremitting pressure. J. B. Jones, the War Department clerk, noted that his boss, James Alexander Seddon, had become gaunt and disheveled—"like a dead man galvanized into muscular action."[39] Davis seemed to be losing sight in his one good eye, and complained of a host of nervous ailments. Judah Benjamin, debonair as ever, floated serenely above the squalor and the fear. Every morning he walked the mile from his house on East Main Street to his office next to Davis's in the old Customs Building. He labored for hours over state papers, and in conference with Davis, and at night, when he did not walk back home, he attended the ladies' "starvation parties" and the gatherings where generals washed the blood and dust off their uniforms to play at *"tableaux vivants."* (Jeb Stuart performed a pilgrim laying a sword at the foot of the Cross.)

Constance Cary Harrison, one of Richmond's leading hostesses, recalled that the secretary of state could always be counted upon to furnish "his charming stories, his dramatic recitations of scraps of verse, and clever comments on men, women and books."[40] In a time of drastic shortages, Benjamin down-shifted his epicureanism into a form of chivalry. He loved anchovy paste, Varina Davis recalled. "He used to say," she later wrote, "with bread made of Crenshaw's flour spread with the paste, English walnuts from an immense tree in the garden, and a glass of the McHenry sherry, of which we had a small store, 'a man's patriotism became rampant.'"[41]

Even at the worst of times, Benjamin never yielded to a bunker mentality, never lost himself in the cause, never forgot about Tennyson and anchovy paste. He remained preoccupied with his family, which had been forced to scatter after Union forces captured New Orleans in 1862. On October 31, 1864, a time when the situation of the South was growing extremely dire, Benjamin sent a leisurely letter to his youngest sister Penina, known as Penny. He had, he said, received letters from "Sis, Hatty and Leah"—three other sisters—and he offered news of each. He continued to send money to Hatty, who had never married. He reported on brother Joe and nephew Lionel (both in the Confederate army). "And now, my darling," he goes on, "I must talk of you and your own precious treasures." How are Ernest and Julius "and my saucy little coquette, Becky?" The note is a reminder that this most self-possessed of all men harbored deep feelings of tenderness that he expressed without restraint only to members of his family.

Jefferson Davis may have cared less about which position Judah Benjamin held than about keeping him in the Cabinet; Varina had been struck at how rapidly the friendship between the two men had advanced during Benjamin's tenure as secretary of war. Nevertheless, by making him secretary of state, Davis had finally placed his friend in the job for which he was plainly best suited, for Benjamin had traveled regularly to Europe for almost twenty years, spoke French and Spanish, and had the bearing and the temperament of a diplomat. Success in foreign capitals mattered almost as much as success on the battlefield, for the long-term survival of the South depended on winning British and French recognition of the Confederacy.

The confidence of early 1861 on that score had evaporated. Both England and France had recognized the Confederacy as a "belligerent" but not as an independent nation; both had agreed to respect the naval blockade that the Union had imposed on Southern ports. Nevertheless, Benjamin would have had good reason to believe that wise statecraft could win over one or both. The Whigs, soon to be known as Liberals, held firm control of the British government, but on most important questions they hardly differed from their Tory rivals. Although the prime minister, Lord Palmerston, had played a leading role in the movement to abolish slavery throughout the Commonwealth, which had succeeded in 1833, he was a deeply conservative figure with an instinctive aversion to the United States. As one of his biographers writes, Palmerston's "fear of democracy outweighed his distaste for slavery."[42]

Palmerston was delighted at the prospect of the dismemberment of the world's largest experiment in democracy; he hoped to forge a thriving trade relationship with a separate Confederacy. The foreign minister, Earl Russell, also instinctively sided with the South. Most remarkable of all was the case of William Gladstone, chancellor of the Exchequer and future Liberal prime minister, soon to be celebrated as "the people's William." Gladstone openly sided with the Confederacy. After Southern victories in the summer of 1862, he delivered a toast in which he declared that the Confederates had made an army and apparently a navy, "and they have made what is more than either—they have made a nation!"[43]

The South may have made a nation, but it had not made a state. The United States had recognized the republics of South America only after they had driven out the armies of Spain in the early 1820s, and thus could be said to have mastered their own fate. The Confederacy, by contrast, was fighting for its existence. Leaving aside questions of conventional practice, recognizing a belligerent, and thus enraging the rump state, constituted a very dangerous wager. William Seward, Lincoln's secretary of state, had vowed that the United States would go to war against any neutral state that recognized the Confederacy even as a belligerent power. Palmerston had responded by sending reinforcements to Canada.

The two nations approached the brink in December 1861, when a Union naval officer stopped a British passenger ship off the coast of Cuba and seized James Mason and John Slidell, the

Confederacy's emissaries to London and Paris. Palmerston demanded the release of the men, and dispatched another three thousand troops to the British garrison in Canada. He told Russell to expect war, and blamed "the rabid hatred of England which animates the exiled Irishmen who direct almost all the Northern newspapers."[44] Seward agreed to release the two men; had he not done so, the outcome of the Civil War could have been very different.

Nevertheless, Palmerston would not act until he felt confident that the South would prevail. Neither he nor Earl Russell would meet with Mason, the Confederate minister. In the late summer of 1862, Russell tersely responded to a long-winded letter from Mason with the observation that England would "acknowledge an independence achieved by victory and maintained by a successful resistance to all attempts to overthrow it." That moment, he added, "has not, in the judgment of Her Majesty's government, yet arrived."[45] Russell also tartly noted that while Mason had written to him that the South could call on twelve million white men, he had been assured by Seward that the correct figure was five million. Mason was a majestic Virginia squire, the grandson of George Mason, a hero of the Continental Congress. He might have been the perfect emissary to the Court of St. James's had he not also been a narrowminded fanatic on slavery. Whatever his personal preferences, Lord Russell put more stock in Seward and Union ambassador Charles Francis Adams than in Mason.

The situation in France appeared more hopeful. A century earlier France had come to the aid of the colonies in their battle for survival against a far more powerful foe; now the South looked to France to defend its demand for independence. After the collapse of the Revolution of 1848, the country had returned to empire under the rule of Napoleon's nephew, Louis Napoleon, an inveterate schemer as well as an ambitious nationalist who aimed to restore the country to its historic role as the dominant force on the Continent. The emperor chafed at British imperial glory and dreamed of reestablishing a French role in the New World by conquering Mexico and installing a European figure as emperor. Once the Civil War ended, Napoleon hoped to join with the Confederacy to overthrow Mexico's ruler, Benito Juárez. The emperor was also no friend of republicanism and recognized in the South a culture sympathetic to hierarchy and traditional authority.

Nevertheless, Louis Napoleon assessed his own position with shrewd dispassion; he knew that he could not afford to alienate England by acting independently on the American dispute. In late March, Mason had written to Judah Benjamin's predecessor, Robert Hunter, that he had repented of his earlier belief that the British Cabinet would take dictation on the question from France; the truth was, in fact, the opposite. "So far, then, as the action of France and England is concerned," he wrote, "we have, I fear, little to hope."[46]

Benjamin had believed that "cotton is king"; he had been wrong. England developed new sources of cotton in India, although they could scarcely replace those in the South, and looked increasingly to the North as a source of wheat. France imported only a tenth as much cotton as did England. Benjamin therefore had no real leverage over either country. Nevertheless, he saw clearly that whatever hopes the Confederacy had lay with France. To Mason in London he sent long and involved arguments about the illegitimacy of the blockade, forlornly hoping that the merits of the case, at least as he understood them, would carry the day, as they had so often in the courtroom. But to his old friend John Slidell, the Confederate commissioner to France, he proposed an audacious deal.

Benjamin authorized Slidell to give France, free of charge, 100,000 bales of cotton, whose landed value in Europe he estimated at $12,500,000—$375 million in today's terms—in exchange for recognition. France could use the funds to build a naval fleet that would allow it to defy the Northern blockade and thus reopen valuable trade routes. The South, in turn, would buy French products, above all small arms and ammunition, with another $8 million or so. "I do not state this as the limit to which you would be authorized to go in making a negotiation on the subject," Benjamin added, "but to place clearly before you the advantage which would result in stipulating for payment in cotton."[47]

Unlike Palmerston or Russell, Louis Napoleon was delighted to meet with the Confederate emissary. He would call for maps and ask Slidell to go minutely over the most recent military campaigns, marveling at the prowess of the great Southern generals and shuddering at the casualty count, which exceeded that of all but the worst battles of his ancestor Napoleon. He never failed to assure his visitor of his ardent sympathy for the Southern cause. In late July, when Slidell came to the Tuileries to present Benjamin's offer, the emperor confessed that in honoring the blockade "he had committed a great error which he now regretted." But nothing now could be done, for "to open their ports forcibly would be an act of war."

The commissioner now played his trump card, laying before Napoleon the lucrative deal that Judah Benjamin had proposed. "It did not seem disagreeable," Slidell wrote home. But the French ruler still balked at breaking the embargo, and insisted that recognition, by itself, could cause France harm while bringing no real value to the South. Not at all, Slidell shot back: Recognition could strengthen the peace party in the North and thus serve the great humanitarian good of ending the desolation of war. The emperor of all the French now put aside the high-minded attitudinizing: "What you say is true," rejoined Louis Napoleon, "but the policy of nations is controlled by their interests, not their sentiments, and ought to be so."[48]

Strange though it seems, Benjamin's diplomacy was stymied not by the doctrinal opposition of two nations that had prohibited slavery, and not even by the intrinsic preference of states for the de facto order, but by realpolitik. The South was the weaker of the two parties; England feared the anger of the Union, and France feared the anger of England. Neither of these fundamental facts would change in the years to come; yet every time the fortunes of war seemed to turn in the South's favor, or some rumor of a change of mood was borne aloft on the current of newsprint or court gossip, either Benjamin or his representatives plunged into a new round of frantic conjecture and desperate planning. Cool reasoning might have told them better; but how could they remain cool when their cause—perhaps their lives—depended on the whims of London and Paris?

The job itself was obviously vastly more congenial to Benjamin than his previous one had been. He no longer had to make split-second decisions upon which the lives of thousands might depend; his emissaries were men very much like himself, including one very close friend; he did not have to serve as the scapegoat for President Davis; and no one questioned his skills at diplomacy. Although it must have wearied him to read endless letters from his commissioner in Brussels, Dudley Mann, who regaled the secretary with all the diplomatic maneuvering of European courts, or from Henry Hotze, a commercial official in London who had secretly started up a magazine and hired English journalists to promote the Southern cause, Benjamin often responded at length. He could not let go of his labored arguments against the blockade or for recognition, little though they availed. He often sent Mason and Slidell detailed accounts of battles won, which they were to repeat in London and Paris to demonstrate that the survival of the Confederacy as an independent nation had become a foregone conclusion.

The sense of inevitable victory shines through Benjamin's letters. Of course he would have conveyed that impression even if he didn't believe it, since the French and British would recognize the South only once victory seemed certain. In the summer of 1862, Benjamin sought to persuade Count Henri Mercier, the French minister to the United States, that, despite everything he had heard in Washington, the South's battlefield victories were irreversible and its capacity to endure losses virtually limitless. He wrote to Slidell that Mercier had left "thoroughly convinced that the war could have no issue but our independence, although he thought it might last a long time."

Benjamin himself didn't think it would last a long time. Between the splendid news from the battlefield and an impending financial crash in the North, he wrote, "our banners will be unfurled before the Potomac in a very short time." How, then, could the European powers continue to withhold recognition? "A refusal by foreign nations now to recognize us," Benjamin wrote, in what Slidell plainly was to regard as talking points, "would surely be far less than simple justice requires and would indicate rather settled aversion than impartial neutrality."[49] Confederate forces had in fact repulsed George McClellan's massive Peninsular Campaign in the late spring and summer of 1862, preserving Richmond itself in the Battle of Seven Days. Yet Benjamin's certitude had an a priori quality to it. After Robert E. Lee's campaign to take the fight to the North suffered a catastrophic reversal at Gettysburg in July 1863, Benjamin could no longer delude himself about Confederate banners waving over the Potomac.

As the bloodshed mounted, and figures on both sides sought some way out of the inferno, Benjamin often fielded visitors from the North bearing potential terms for an armistice. Soon after Gettysburg, Lincoln himself authorized Issachar Zacharie, a Southern Jew, a flamboyant self-promoter, and the president's personal chiropodist, to make a secret visit to Richmond bearing peace plans. On September 27, 1863, he met with the senior members of Davis's cabinet. Zacharie proposed to return the South to the Union in exchange for a gradual, and compensated, emancipation of the slaves. Benjamin replied flatly that the South could accept no terms that did not guarantee "self-government." The episode does not quite end there. That night Zacharie and Benjamin met alone. Lincoln's emissary had extensive ties to the Jewish community in New Orleans, and had served as a Union spy there earlier that year. He might have had personal intelligence that Benjamin could not have learned from anyone else. The next day Zacharie wrote Benjamin a startling, treacly letter, though this was not out of character for him. "I was so excited last night," the chiropodist wrote, "and overcome at the pleasure of meeting you, knowing that the confederate flag was waving over my head, that my heart was bursting with joy."[50] Had Zacharie not been such a gross flatterer, one would take this for treachery. There is a third possibility. In closing, the emissary expressed the hope that Benjamin "would never regret the interview we had last night." Some scholars have seen in this rather moist *envoi* a reference to a homosexual tryst.[51] It could be; yet Benjamin had good reason to wish to meet with Zacharie alone, and fawning was second nature to Zacharie.

Benjamin was prepared to meet these peace offerings with a stern rebuff, despite the reverses on the field, because, like Davis, he felt absolutely certain of the South's moral as of its martial superiority. In his diplomatic correspondence Benjamin never failed to repeat, and magnify, instances of Northern abuses, which he considered monstrous. He consigned Union generals to the lowest level of Hell. The harsh regime that General Butler, known as the "Beast," had imposed on Benjamin's beloved New Orleans in May 1862 had shown the world the Union's true colors. Butler was a vicious anti-Semite who regarded Jews as foreigners who naturally supported the Confederacy against the Union, and "who all deserve at the hands of the Government what is due to the Jew Benjamin, Slidell, Mallory and Floyd"—hanging, presumably. Occupying troops turned Benjamin's sisters out of the family house, though not before the women had managed to remove most of their valuables. In a letter to Slidell, Benjamin passed over these abuses, instead assuring his friend that Butler really had, as word had it, instructed his men to treat the ladies of New Orleans as "women of the town pursuing their avocation." In the mind of the secretary of state, it was the very perfidy of the Union that made the failure of the Southern cause unthinkable. He was, he wrote to Mason in 1863, "entirely confident of our ability to resist for an indefinite period the execrable savages who are now murdering and plundering our people."[52]

Yet it was becoming all too plain that the cost of that resistance would be almost unbearable. Thirty-four hundred Confederate soldiers had died at Antietam; another seven thousand had been wounded. More than five thousand were killed and wounded at Fredericksburg. What kind of South would emerge from such carnage? If the North would not retire on its own, only diplomatic intervention could bring the war to an early end. In October 1862, Louis Napoleon, always seeking a means to insert France into the British preserve of North America, told Slidell that he planned to call for joint mediation by France, Russia, and England to negotiate a six-month cease-fire preliminary to a negotiated end to the war. Davis agreed to the plan, and in December Benjamin instructed Slidell to remind senior French officials that the South would immediately need $300 million worth of goods—textiles, iron and steel, leather goods and clothing, glass, and crockery. Should the war end without European intercession, Slidell should add, Northern merchants would flock southward and monopolize that vast trade before France or England could react.[53]

The Palmerston government seriously considered the peace bid. Deadlocked, the government agreed once again to await the outcome on the battlefield. While the cabinet deliberated, Charles Francis Adams, Lincoln's minister in London, stated plainly that the North would not accept a cease-fire that would only embolden the peace party in the North. Seward asserted that there were "no Northern and Southern states," but only "an insurrectionary party" originating in the South.[54] President Lincoln would not sit down with the Confederacy as an equal party; hostilities would end when the South returned to the Union. The proposed peace talks collapsed before they could get off the ground.

The question of slavery barely arose in the Confederacy's diplomatic relations with European powers for the first two years of the war. Not only the Liberals in the British Cabinet but most of the gentlemen of high rank in London treated slavery as a matter to be adjudicated between the warring American sides. While virtually all Frenchmen of note regarded slavery as a grotesque violation of the revolutionary principle of human equality, that category did not include the most powerful Frenchman of all, Louis Napoleon. At the end of a long conversation in 1862, the emperor asked John Slidell "whether we anticipated no difficulty from our slaves." Slidell said that "they had never been more quiet and respectful." And that, he informed Benjamin with obvious satisfaction, "was the only allusion made to slavery during the interview."[55]

That all too tactful silence became more difficult to maintain after Lincoln published the Emancipation Proclamation on September 22, 1862, and then issued it in final form January 1, 1863. The Proclamation freed few slaves, for Lincoln insisted on exempting those held in Southern areas now controlled by the Union, for fear of provoking a rebellion among whites, but it fundamentally changed the nature of the conflict. "The cause of the slaves and the cause of the country," Frederick Douglass declared, was now one and the same.[56] This was precisely the view that took root in progressive middle-class circles in England. Anti-slavery societies formed across the country and convened immense rallies addressed by the nation's leading speakers. Townships and municipalities passed resolutions to send congratulatory messages to Washington. The great Radical leader Richard Cobden wrote to Charles Sumner to report that the surge of popular enthusiasm "closed the mouths of those who have been advocating the side of the South."

Although midcentury England was very far from a democracy, the government could not afford to be indifferent to mass opinion. In November 1862, Mason reported that he had heard from a senior official that the Palmerston government would not recognize the South even in the aftermath of victory unless it banned the slave trade; nor, he was told, would a Tory government. The standing of the Confederacy in France was yet more compromised. Edwin de Leon, a member of a prominent South Carolina Jewish family whom Davis and Benjamin had sent to Europe to act as a secret propaganda agent, wrote to Benjamin to say that, the emperor's own feelings notwithstanding, France would no longer consider recognizing the Confederacy absent "some promise for prospective emancipation." The "old cry of slavery," a resigned de Leon wrote, had become "the real *bête noire* of the French imagination."[57]

Henry Hotze, now moving between France and England, wrote in September 1863 to report that in Europe, and above all France, "there are no such violent anti-slavery demonstrations as in England, simply because there is no one against whom to make them." Like atheism, he added, the defense of slavery was regarded as too indecent for polite conversation. Hotze had heard rumors that the South planned to arm 500,000 slaves to supplement its own forces. He hoped that wasn't so, yet the Confederacy "must confront anti-slavery sentiment."[58]

Benjamin didn't have to be told. He assured Hotze that he had come to the same conclusion about French public opinion from reading the press, above all the *Revue des Deux Mondes*. His tone, as always, was measured, but Benjamin seemed to write himself into a state composed equally of fury and despair. The slave uprising in Haiti seventy years earlier, and the accompanying slaughter of whites, he observed, "does not seem in the least to disturb the faith of these philanthropists in the entire justice and policy of a war waged for this end, and our resistance to the fate proposed for us is treated as a crime against liberty and civilization." But French hypocrisy paled before British cynicism. "Our judgment is now finally made up that the British cabinet deemed it best for Great Britain that some hundreds of thousands of human beings should be slaughtered on this continent that her people might reap profit and become more powerful." Even when Benjamin's hopes wavered, his sense of righteousness never did.[59]

The rumors of a draft that had reached Hotze still amounted to nothing more than whispers, despite growing fears over a shortage of white manpower. The Confederate Congress had no competency on issues of slavery, which belonged to the states. In any case, as Benjamin observed in response to a letter in August 1863 advocating such a policy, the cost of buying the slaves from owners would be prohibitive, while the economic consequences of losing their farm labor would be catastrophic.[60] Yet it was clear that for reasons both logistical and diplomatic, the issue could not be put off forever.

From its first years, the Confederacy had developed a network of agents engaged in intelligence, espionage, and sabotage. Both the War Department and the State Department operated their own "secret service," with agents passing between the groups or borrowed from the intelligence operatives working for General Winder, the police chief. Benjamin probably would have been privy to all of the South's secret operations, but he was directly responsible only for his own spies. Edwin de Leon later wrote that Benjamin and Davis had sent him to Paris with "full secret instructions, but did not label and advertise me."[61] He reported back to Benjamin that he had doled out bribes to French journalists to advocate the Southern cause.

(Henry Hotze would later observe that French journalists were more biddable than the English journalists he had hired.)

Benjamin fired de Leon in early 1864, concluding that he had accomplished very little while managing to jeopardize the work of his actual minister, John Slidell. Benjamin also sent two secret agents to Ireland—one of them a Catholic priest—with instructions to stop the flow of Irishmen emigrating in order to enlist in (and be paid by) the Union army. They did not succeed.

By early 1864, Benjamin was still sounding the same note of resolute optimism that he had earlier. In a dispatch to Slidell in April, he wrote, "I never felt a more sincere conviction than I now entertain that the year 1864 will witness our honorable welcome into the family of nations." He now understood that neither France nor England would intervene to bring the war to an end. Yet he was convinced that the North was losing the will to fight. He also wrote to Slidell—again, for dissemination in Paris—that "the fierce and passionate dissensions which are being daily developed among the Northern people" almost guaranteed a quick end to the war.

There were rumors that Lincoln would not run for reelection, or that the Democrats would nominate a peace candidate. This opened up to Benjamin a new phase of secret action. By this time a number of Confederate officers and sympathizers had established themselves in Canada, where, thanks to British sympathy with their cause, they could operate free from interference.

In March, Benjamin asked the Virginian A. II. H. Stuart, a former secretary of the interior, to meet with him and the president. They asked Stuart to go to Canada in order to secretly support a growing movement in the North, and especially in the West, to bring the war to an end. They had, they said, deposited three million pounds in London—an immense sum for the straitened Confederacy—in order to finance the operation.

It was to be a domestic version of the propaganda campaign they had funded in France and Europe. Stuart regarded the idea as fanciful and declined the offer.

Benjamin would not be denied. His self-righteousness had so warped his judgment that when he looked to the North he saw only battle fatigue and bankruptcy. As he wrote to John Slidell in Paris, "It is difficult to perceive how in the present state of Northern finances and the fierce and passionate dissensions which are being daily developed among the Northern people, it can be possible to carry on the war many months longer."[62] With a sharp push, Benjamin thought, Lincoln's political support could collapse, allowing an anti-war Democrat to win the upcoming presidential election. His agents would administer that push. Benjamin now turned to Jacob Thompson, also a former interior secretary, who agreed to take up the mission. In the last days of April, Benjamin authorized Thompson to receive from the Treasury $1 million in gold. Thompson promptly left for Canada, where he would be joined by a former U.S. senator, Clement C. Clay, and a stream of Confederate officers and others whom Benjamin sent north. The war effort had entered a new realm of political subversion.

Once in Canada, Thompson made contact with members of the Sons of Liberty, a secret society of Northerners opposed to the war effort. (They were also known as Copperheads, for the copper coins they carried as tokens of membership.) In July, Thompson sent a breathless dispatch to Benjamin claiming that the order had 85,000 members in Illinois, 56,000 in Indiana, and 40,000 in Ohio. Thompson planned to finance a movement among them to nominate an anti-war candidate at the Democratic Convention being held in Chicago that summer. But the group's leaders had already concluded that Lincoln would only emerge stronger from the election, and Thompson instead acceded to their plans to carry out acts of sabotage during the party convention in Chicago.

When the convention was postponed from early July to late August, the men fixed August 16th as the day of action. "The plan is this," Thompson wrote. "Instantaneously a movement will be made at Chicago, Rock Island and Springfield"— the site of prisons holding Confederate soldiers. "These places will be seized and held, the prisoners released, armed and mounted, 7000 at Chicago, 9000 at Rock Island." Rebels would seize the government in Indiana. "If Indiana and Ohio will move they will constitute themselves a western Confederacy and demand peace (and if peace is not demanded, it shall be war to the knife)."[63] Thompson never received approval from Benjamin for this audacious plan. Indeed, since Benjamin later complained at the end of the year that he had never heard from Thompson, it is quite possible that the dispatch was seized before it could reach Richmond. (It nevertheless survived in Confederate archives.) Benjamin might have considered the scheme hare-brained, or even morally wrong. In any case, Thompson apparently felt that he had carte blanche to spend the money as he saw fit. He paid for 4,000 pistols and 135,000 rounds of ammunition to be sent to Chicago, site of the convention.

Everything began to go wrong as the date approached. First the men lost heart and decided to await the outcome of the election. Only twenty-five conspirators showed up in Chicago. What's more, a Union spy, Felix Grundy Stidger, had insinuated himself into the highest ranks of the Indiana Sons of Liberty, and exposed their plans.[64] The plots in Indiana and Kentucky were scotched, and several conspirators were arrested. Federal troops descended on Chicago, seized the weapons and ammunition, and arrested three of the plotters.[65]

The designs of Thompson and his team grew more feverish, and more violent, as the fortunes of the South declined. They failed as abjectly as the earlier ones had. In early December, Thompson wrote Benjamin a nineteen-page letter in which he detailed, and tried to palliate, the colossal waste of the Confederacy's precious funds. In September, several of his agents tried to steal the steamer *Michigan* and pilot it to Johnson's Island, in Lake Erie off the coast of Ohio, where they would attack a stockade and free the Confederate soldiers held there, including senior Confederate officers. At the last minute, the men declined to attack the ship, much less the very well guarded federal prison. Plans to lay siege to other prisons had to be abandoned when surveillance showed them to be too well guarded. The charmingly named "Mr. Major Minor" promised to burn federal steamers in the Mississippi, and in fact did so—but then bragged about it and had to go into hiding. Thompson also gave money to a Mr. Churchill to burn down Cincinnati, and was still waiting for news at the time of the letter.

Thompson also wrote that, all else having failed, he agreed to a plan to burn down New York City on Election Day, November 8. This project was all too well telegraphed. In mid-October, the *Richmond Whig* ran an editorial urging the South to burn down a major American city in response to Grant's orders to his commanders to burn Southern grain stocks. Ten thousand Union soldiers entered New York in advance of the election. The saboteurs fled north, regrouped, and returned several weeks later. On November 25, the chief conspirator, James Headley, picked up from a clandestine chemist a heavy valise filled with bottles of a phosphorous-based chemical known as "Greek fire" that ignited on exposure to air. Headley and his gang attempted to burn down hotels in lower Manhattan in the hopes that a conflagration would consume the city. It appears, however, that they did not understand that the chemical required oxygen as a fuel, and would not spread from a closed hotel room. The city's fire department quickly doused all the flames.[66]

Thompson sought to put this fiasco in the best light. "I do not think my mission has been altogether fruitless," he wrote. "The masses remain, true, brave and I believe willing." The selection of a new leadership cadre of the Sons of Liberty "is now going forward with great vigor and success."[67] Benjamin disagreed, and ordered Thompson home.

Benjamin thought that he was paying for an influence campaign, not an insurrection. Would he have paid for one if he thought it would succeed? In a letter to Francis Lawley, I. Q. Washington, Benjamin's private secretary, wrote that he had been present at his boss's meeting with Thompson, and "there was not a word or a thought that looked to any violations of the rules of war, as they exist, among civilized nations."[68] That, of course, came after the fact; but we also have contemporary evidence of Benjamin's sense of what was acceptable in war. In a dispatch he sent in 1863 to Lieutenant J. J. Capston, one of his agents in Ireland, he forbade illegal or even morally questionable methods: Your actions, Benjamin admonished, "are to be confined to such as are strictly legitimate, honorable and proper. We rely on truth and justice alone. . . . the means employed must be such as this government may fearlessly avow and openly justify, if your conduct should ever be called into question."[69]

Judah Benjamin kept his cool even after General William Tecumseh Sherman seized Atlanta in September 1864. The secretary of state wrote to Henry Hotze to marvel at how the North "magnifies the results of a successful skirmish into a grand victory that has 'broken the back of the rebellion.'" The South had greeted the event with nonchalance, he reported— perhaps a sign of "the innate consciousness of the superiority of the Southern race."[70] He was not being ironical; he really did believe that the South had deeper reserves of fortitude and discipline than did the more pampered souls of the North; in any case the survival of the cause had become so fixed a postulate for Benjamin that it was now apparently immune to contrary information. But Lincoln's reelection showed that the North was far more prepared to prolong the fight than Benjamin had imagined. Sherman began his pitiless "March to the Sea" immediately after the election, laying waste to much of Georgia on his way to taking Savannah. Benjamin's tone shifted from lofty and complacent to bitter and desperate. "There can be no doubt," he wrote wildly to Slidell, that the North's "settled ulterior purpose" was "to attack England as soon as disengaged from the struggle with us."[71] The Confederacy was fighting France and England's war—couldn't the Europeans see that?

The question of slavery, which a year earlier Benjamin had felt he could afford to put off, now became paramount. In early 1864, Major General Patrick Cleburne, a highly regarded commander known as "the Stonewall of the west," had gathered together the senior officers of the Army of Tennessee and proposed arming the slaves in exchange for a promise of freedom. Whatever his personal feelings, Jefferson Davis knew that he had no chance of winning approval for such a plan from the Confederate Congress. He made sure the proposal never saw the light of day. But by fall 1864, others began to echo the call. In October, the Richmond *Sentinel* wrote that the time had come "to enlist the negro element on our side." But to do what? Lee had come to accept that slaves could take over the tasks of manual labor then being performed by soldiers—but not to bear arms.

In November, Davis used the occasion of his annual address to Congress to discuss the role of slaves in the war effort. The president's legalistic rhetoric, and his blurring of once solid lines over the question of slavery, sounds much more like Benjamin than Davis himself. The slave, Davis explained, skirting the edge of the permissible, has a dual character, as both "property" and "person." Heretofore the state had temporarily seized the slave-as-property from their owners in order to perform specified acts of labor. The time had come, he said, for the state to purchase the slaves for full-time work, and thus to claim entire control over their personhood. The distinction seemed unnecessary, and was not one to which slave owners were accustomed. But Davis, or Benjamin, had a further purpose. Once become owner, Davis continued, the state would have to decide "by what tenure he should be held." If in perpetual servitude, how could slaves be induced to perform work that requires "loyalty and zeal" save by the promise of freedom? Should they, then, be freed straightaway? Davis proposed a middle course, a pledge of emancipation on discharge from duties. But like Lee, the Confederate president was not yet prepared to publicly advocate the arming of slaves, which well might lead to "incitement of the same persons to insurrection against their masters." So grave a decision could be justified only if the alternative was "subjugation."[72]

Southerners had fought the war in order to protect the right of states to enslave black people. With their backs to the wall, they now had to consider the possibility that the continuation of slavery would doom the survival of the cause. They had always defended secession with the language of states' rights. Yet it was slavery that had made the South what it was. Davis had sought to lay out a middle path, in which slaves might gain their freedom through service to the cause without ever bearing arms. His unwillingness to do so arose not simply from a prudent fear of revolt. As Howell Cobb, Georgia's leading political figure, grimly observed, "If slaves will make good soldiers, our whole theory of slavery is wrong."[73] Should the Confederacy survive by arming the slaves, it would have to reconsider its very reason for being. How would it live on the other side of that choice?

Unlike Davis, or Cobb, or most Southern leaders, Benjamin was prepared to choose survival over slavery—or rather, he was convinced earlier than they were that the choice had to be made. In late December he urged a correspondent in Charleston who had advocated arming the slaves to convert local editors to the cause. Benjamin wrote that he had seen the moment coming "for a year past"—which is to say that his professions of optimism in the middle of 1864 should not be taken altogether at face value. He agreed with his correspondent, Charles Porcher, that "the negroes will certainly be made to fight against us if not armed for our defense." And if they are to fight for the freedom of the South, "they are entitled to their own" liberty—not in the remote future, but right away. Those were the terms on which slaves would agree to fight.

What followed from this heretical thought? Should slavery simply come to an end? Must Southern whites live with blacks as fellow citizens? The prospect could not be squared with "our faith in the doctrine that the negro is an inferior race." Yet it must have seemed to Benjamin too late in the day to propose, as moderates North and South like Henry Clay and Lincoln himself had, that former slaves be exported to a "colony," presumably Sierra Leone on Africa's west coast. A masterful threader of logical needles, Benjamin suggested "cautious legislation" to emancipate the families of freedmen "after an intermediate stage of serfage or peonage." At the conclusion of this tutelage, ex-slaves would enjoy "certain rights of property" and "a certain degree of personal liberty" as well as "legal protection for the marital and personal relations."[74] Benjamin seemed to be anticipating the Jim Crow laws passed after Reconstruction.

For Benjamin, emancipation was a diplomatic question as much as a tactical one. Before the end of the year he sent Duncan Kenner, his friend and lodger on Main Street, to Paris and London. Benjamin had wanted Kenner to offer immediate emancipation in exchange for recognition, but Davis was not prepared to go that far. Kenner's instructions authorized him to offer abolition "in a fair and reasonable time."[75] Kenner made his way to New York through the Northern blockade and boarded a ship bound for Paris.

In the summer of 1864, forces under General Ulysses Grant had managed to cross the James River to the east of Richmond, then march south to Petersburg, the chief rail junction south of Richmond. By the end of the year, both armies were observing a winter pause; but the Confederacy had lost one major city after another—first Atlanta, then Nashville, then Savannah. Only Richmond remained. Lee had somehow staved off one attack after another, but his men were running out of food, ammunition, and clothing; thousands had deserted. Lee finally accepted the conscription of slaves as soldiers.

Benjamin then urged Davis to use the support of the revered commander to call for the Congress to authorize the policy. According to Varina Davis, who said she was listening to the Cabinet meeting in the next room, as was probably her habit, Benjamin pressed Davis to issue the call at a public meeting in order to "feel the pulse of the people."[76] Davis finally understood that the prospect of "subjugation" was at hand. He not only agreed to Benjamin's proposition, but either asked him to deliver the speech or acquiesced to his wish to do so. This would constitute Benjamin's supreme act as presidential heat shield.

The mass meeting was held February 9 at the African Church, where slaves and free blacks worshiped. As the largest space in the city, it was commandeered by white leaders at their convenience. Now, in a bizarre irony, white Richmond would use the church in order to determine the destiny of their slaves without, of course, asking the slaves themselves. Attendance was estimated at 10,000 both inside the church, where ladies had lined up for a seat hours earlier, and on the steps and the sidewalk outside. Benjamin rose to speak in public as a Confederate official for the very first time—and for the last. He had barely exercised his sublime gift for oratory since he had left Congress four years before. No speech he had ever given mattered so much as this one, for the survival of the Confederacy seemed to hang in the balance. Few in the audience had any idea what the secretary of state planned to say; most would not have welcomed the news. Benjamin understood that he had to seduce the crowd with logic even as he showed that he shared their blazing faith in the cause. He had to carry them with him to a place they did not want to go.

Benjamin began by flattering his listeners' patriotism, pride, honor, self-sacrifice. "We now know," he said, "in the core of our hearts, that this people must conquer its freedom or die." He then turned, ever so slowly, to his real subject. "We want means," Benjamin said. "Are they in this country? If so, they belong to the country, and not to the man who chances to hold them now. . . . I now ask, has any man the right to hold a bale of cotton from his country?" The crowded shouted back, "No!" As with cotton, Benjamin went on, slowly tightening the noose of logic, so with tobacco. And bacon, too. "I want one other thing," Benjamin cried. "War is a game that cannot be played without men." The soldiers manning the trenches at Petersburg needed reinforcement.

Benjamin still wasn't ready to raise the curtain on his shocking proposition. "I will now call your attention to some figures which I wish you to seriously ponder," he said, very much as he would have to a judge on the bench hearing one of his insurance cases. The North "brought out 3,000,000 men against 1,664,000 Confederates, who lived in the beginning of the war to draw sword in their country's service. . . . Our resources of white population have greatly diminished, but you have 680,000 black men of the same ages." Only now, having fully prepared the ground, did Benjamin state the case: "Let us say to every negro who wishes to go into the ranks on condition of being made free, 'Go and fight—you are free.'"[77] Was this not precisely the advantage that the North had seized with the Emancipation Proclamation? "Let us imitate them in this," Benjamin declared. "I would imitate them in nothing else."[78]

Benjamin had had the crowd in the palm of his hands until that moment. Now one cried "No! Never!" while another shouted "Send in the slaves!" Benjamin had posed the existential question, as Davis felt that even he could not. The secretary of state had directed to himself the rancor of the bitter-enders. The Confederate Congress considered a resolution stating, "Judah P. Benjamin is not a wise and prudent Secretary of State and lacks the confidence of the country." Members divided evenly on the question. Benjamin promptly wrote out a letter of resignation. He suggested that Davis ask himself, "Will your administration be strengthened or any opposition to it disarmed by substituting another in my place in the Cabinet?" Davis, predictably, ignored the question, and retained his confidant.

Benjamin, however, had nothing left to do. The Duncan Kenner mission had come to nothing; Lord Palmerston had ruled out recognition of the Confederacy under any circumstances. The Confederate Congress dithered over Benjamin's proposal until finally producing a watered-down compromise that attracted only a handful of slave volunteers. By the middle of March, the 50,000 Confederate troops manning the picket lines at Petersburg, hungry, ragged, and desperately low on ammunition, faced 125,000 Union soldiers under General Grant who would soon be reinforced by 50,000 men marching south from the Shenandoah Valley. On March 25, Lee ordered a desperate breakout attempt; his forces lost 4,000 men and were forced to retreat still farther toward Richmond. On April 1, Grant attacked at the Battle of Five Forks, and the South took another 10,000 casualties. President Davis and his commanding general had already agreed that if Grant appeared poised to break through the lines, both the Army of the Potomac and the civilian government would abandon Richmond and regroup at Danville, 125 miles to the southwest. Lee had believed that he could hold out until mid-April. Now he understood that he had been too optimistic.

April 2 was a Sunday, a fine, sunny day in Richmond. Jefferson Davis attended church, as he always did, at St. Patrick's, the Episcopal church adjacent to the Capitol Building and the Customs House, seat of the Confederate government. In the middle of the service, the sextant, William Irving, tapped Davis on the shoulder and handed him a message. Those sitting nearby saw the Confederate president go pale. The message, from Lee, said that Grant had broken through the lines and was heading for Richmond. The general added, "I advise that appropriate preparations be made for leaving Richmond tonight."[79] What ought to have been an orderly withdrawal would become a frantic retreat. Davis rose, returned to the Customs House and summoned his cabinet. He told them to prepare to abandon the city.

Whatever he said in public, Benjamin was always ready to assume, and prepare for, the worst. He had already sent both personal effects and state papers south with a clerk. His Confederate currency would be useless, but he gathered several thousand dollars worth of gold—presumably his own, though perhaps requisitioned from the Treasury. He began destroying state papers, above all documents related to the secret service. (The Treasury records, showing disbursements, survived.) At two o'clock he summoned the French consul, Alfred Paul, and bade him farewell. "Mr. Benjamin," Paul reported back to his minister, "said to me in a trembling voice, 'I have nothing in particular to say to you, but I wanted to be sure to shake your hand before my departure.'" Benjamin would no more relax his guard before the consul than he would before the cabinet. The precipitate leave-taking, he said, "is simply a measure of prudence. I hope that we will return in a few weeks." The plan on which Davis and Lee agreed did, in fact, foresee a return to Richmond after Lee and General Johnston had somehow routed Union forces to the south; but it is unlikely that Benjamin put much stock in such fever dreams. Paul was left wondering if he had just witnessed an example of Benjamin's "persisting illusion" or his "lack of sincerity."[80]

Richmond was in tumult. The banks opened at 2 p.m. and customers scrambled to remove their cash and valuables. Ladies sewed their jewelry into belts to wear under their dresses. Wagons were piled high with goods; those with money were prepared to pay anything for a carriage. Soldiers were ordered to destroy the stores and the ammunition. The Union spy Elizabeth Van Lew wrote: "The constant explosion of shells, the blowing up of gunboats, and of the powder magazine, seemed to jar, to shake the earth, and lend a mighty language to the scene."[81] Davis had ordered a departure for 7 p.m., and the cabinet assembled at the railway station. The entire Confederate treasury—$528,000 worth of silver and gold—had been loaded on a separate train guarded by sixty soldiers. But Jefferson Davis would not leave. He stood by the telegrapher's station hoping, with what must have increasingly felt like a lunatic fixity, for news that the tide had turned. Finally, at 11, he boarded the train, and it slowly moved off for Danville. As the train crossed the James River, sappers blew up the bridge to keep Grant's men from using it to pursue the government-in-exile.

Every member of the Confederate government, save Davis himself, understood that the cause had failed. But alone among them, Judah Benjamin knew that if he once fell—if he were captured—he would fall forever, as Benét would later put it, like the rejected stone.

5

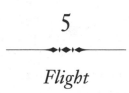

Flight

THE RAILROAD CARS carrying the government of the Confederacy passed through Virginia in the dead of night. The men inside must have been weary and very close to despair. They had expected to abandon Richmond—but not so suddenly, or under such dire conditions. Only one among them kept up his spirits. Navy Secretary Stephen Mallory was startled to observe the irrepressible secretary of state, "his pleasant smile, his mild Havana, and the very twirl of his slender gold-headed cane contributing to . . . the careless confidence of the last man outside the ark, who assured Noah of his belief that, 'it would not be such a h- - - of a shower, after all.'"[1]

This was the same brave face that Benjamin had turned to the French consul earlier in the day: in the role that he had assigned himself as master of all circumstances, he would maintain at all times an almost superhuman sang-froid. Perhaps he was performing for his brother-in-law Jules, whom he had somehow connived to bring with him on the train. It was the role to which, in any case, his temperament was suited. When Varina had once asked her friend about the source of his equanimity, he had explained "that he believed there was a fate in the destiny of nations, and it was wrong and useless to distress one's self and thus weaken one's energy to bear what was foreordained to happen."[2] That was misleading only insofar as it implied a stoical resignation; Benjamin would never be passive in the face of misfortune.

Lee's forces had redeployed to the west, where they expected to find a new supply of rations as they headed toward North Carolina. But there was no food at Amelia Court House, the designated depot, and Lee was forced to stop while his men foraged and Union forces under General Philip Sheridan moved to block his passage. Meanwhile, portions of Richmond had been engulfed by flames from tobacco warehouses put to the torch, lest this valuable source of currency fall into Yankee hands. The streets filled with Union soldiers who lowered the Confederate standard and rang up the Stars and Stripes. President Lincoln himself arrived April 4. Black men and women flung themselves at the feet of the Great Emancipator—who bade them kneel not to him but only to God, who had delivered them.

Nevertheless, the Confederacy remained officially intact. In Jefferson Davis's mind, increasingly unhinged from reality, the cause had suffered only a temporary reversal. On April 5, after a meeting of the Cabinet, he instructed Benjamin to write out and deliver a message to the editor of the *Danville Register*. "We have now entered a new phase of our struggle the memory of which is to endure for all ages," the missive read. "Relieved from the necessity of guarding cities and particular points, important but not vital to your defense . . . nothing is now needed to render our triumph certain but the exhibition of our own unquenchable resolve. Let us but will it, and we are free."[3]

On April 9, his force surrounded, his men starving and exhausted, Lee sought out Grant at Appomattox Court House to negotiate terms of surrender. But Davis refused to regard this shattering moment as the death knell of the Confederacy. Instead he ordered the Cabinet to evacuate once again, this time for Greensboro, North Carolina, though no one in the city had expected or prepared for the arrival of the government-in-exile. A hard rain had fallen, and men and horses plunged knee-deep in mud, while straggling soldiers fought to clamber aboard the presidential train. Now joined by Generals Beauregard and Johnston, Davis convened the Cabinet once again. The generals observed that they were outnumbered in the field, 350,000 to 25,000. Davis still refused to accept defeat. The next morning, Johnston pressed the case for surrender, bluntly telling Davis, "our people are tired of war, feel themselves whipped and will not fight." Johnston was joined by all the Cabinet members—save one. Judah Benjamin, Johnston later wrote, "made a speech for war much like Sempronius in Addison's play"—a reference to a character in the eighteenth-century work *Cato* who cries out, "Gods! can a Roman senate long debate / Which of the two to choose, slavery or death!"[4]

Perhaps one should say that Benjamin's final act of political oratory was not the speech at the African Church but this astonishing address to a dozen men, all of them accustomed to regarding the secretary of state as the firmly fixed arm of the Confederate compass. They must have been staggered, not to mention very dismayed, to hear this polished courtier rattling his saber on behalf of a suicidal cause. Though he had told his host in Danville that he would "never be taken alive," Benjamin shared none of Davis's yearning for martyrdom. Nor did he share Davis's lunatic faith in some looming military salvation. Yet Benjamin may have understood that Davis could not survive without his illusions; appearing to share them may have been the final act that this grateful servant could perform for his king. He would be loyal to the last—or almost.

Davis and his entourage continued to flee south, toward Charlotte. The marauding soldiers of Union General George Stoneman had cut the railway lines and threatened to capture the Confederate government. The men pushed through the mud on horseback. Benjamin, uncomfortable in the saddle, made do with a horse-drawn ambulance, in which he rode with several others, including Jules. At one point Burton Harrison, Davis's aide-de-camp, rode back to see what had become of the group and found that their vehicle had gotten stuck in a muddy ditch. Harrison later recalled that he "could see from afar the occasional bright glow of Benjamin's cigar." As he drew closer, Harrison was astonished to hear the secretary of state's "silvery voice" as he "rhythmically intoned, for their comfort, verse after verse of Tennyson's 'Ode on the Death of the Duke of Wellington,'" which, like much of Tennyson, he knew by heart.[5] If he couldn't do anything to remedy the disaster—that was not within his sphere of competence—Benjamin could at least beguile his fellow sufferers until help arrived, which it eventually did.

It may have been that very evening—the timing of the trip is unclear—that John Wilkes Booth entered Abraham Lincoln's box in the upper tier of Ford's Theater and murdered him. The Davis party learned the news when it reached Charlotte. The Confederate leaders had been marked men before, but now they might be accused not just of treason but of the assassination of the president. With Booth himself shifting among safe houses in Virginia, suspicion immediately fell on the Canadian secret service operation, which had already carried out terrorist attacks, and on the civilian leadership in Richmond, above all Davis and Benjamin, who exercised direct responsibility over Jacob Thompson and his Canadian operatives. Benjamin's Jewishness unleashed ancient prejudices. Murdered on Good Friday, Abraham Lincoln underwent an instant transfiguration: he was Jesus Christ, crucified for the national sin of slavery. And who had "parted the garments" of Our Lord? The Jews. Benjamin understood very well that, if captured, Jefferson Davis would be granted the full majesty of the law, while he himself might well be hanged from the nearest tree.

Was there any shred of truth to the claim of a broader conspiracy? Benjamin and Booth were connected through the person of John Surratt, a wraithlike figure whom Benjamin employed to slip back and forth through Union lines as a messenger. Booth met Surratt in December 1864, recruited him into his ring, and used his mother's inn as a safe house both before and after the assassination. But no evidence emerged either that Booth had ever met or communicated with Davis or Benjamin—or even visited Richmond—or that Surratt had spoken to Benjamin or other Confederate leaders of the planned assassination, which in any case Booth did not put into operation until after the civilian government fled.

In the course of the investigation following Lincoln's death, Samuel Conover, a former clerk in the Confederate War Department, testified that Jacob Thompson had sought to recruit him into the assassination plot. He also asserted that he had been present when John Surratt had reached Thompson's office between April 6th and 9th with letters from Davis and Benjamin. After perusing the documents, Conover said, Thompson tapped them and said, "This makes the thing all right." But it later turned out that "Conover" was, in fact, another man, Charles Dunham, who had nourished a burning hatred for Davis after the latter had sentenced him to six months in a Confederate prison.[6] Benjamin's biographers are united in treating the allegation against Benjamin as a cynical act of vengeance by enraged Union officials; the most thorough of them, Eli Evans, regards the claim almost as a blood libel.

Many details of the Confederate secret services are known

today that were hidden from federal prosecutors; other facts have emerged only in the last few decades. In his 1892 memoir, *A Confederate Spy*, Thomas Conrad, a Virginia cavalry officer and chaplain, described in detail his failed plot to kidnap Lincoln in the fall of 1864. In September, Conrad came to Richmond, where he met with Secretary of War James Seddon— in order, Conrad later wrote, to work out the details of the kidnapping plot. Conrad said that he also met with Davis, who directed Benjamin to draw funds for the venture. In a letter to Seddon, Conrad said that Benjamin had ordered $400 in gold to be withdrawn for him. Records of the Confederate Treasury, discovered only about twenty years ago, confirm both the timing and the sum of the withdrawal.

Conrad reached Washington in late September and began, he wrote, "to reconnoiter the White House" from a stand of trees in Lafayette Park. He decided to seize the president on his way to the Soldier's Home, the summer residence to which Lincoln often traveled alone. But Conrad and his team had to back off when they found Lincoln accompanied by a cavalry detachment. Conrad spent the ensuing months laying the groundwork for another attempt. The authors of *Come Retribution*, an elaborately detailed study of Confederate plots on Lincoln, conclude that Conrad's plot ultimately merged with that of Booth, whose own plan to kidnap Lincoln came to naught in March 1865. The authors, however, are not able to convincingly tie Booth to officials in Richmond.[7]

It is possible, though hardly likely, that Seddon, but not Jefferson Davis or Judah Benjamin, knew why Conrad was being paid. If the latter two did know, we must ask why they felt justified in kidnapping Lincoln and what they hoped to get from it. The answer to the first may lie with a Union raid on Richmond in early March 1864; when a senior figure, Colonel Ulric Dahlgren, was killed, a note was found in his uniform that read, "once in the city, it must be destroyed and Jeff Davis and his cabinet killed." The note (which has since been judged authentic) enraged Southern opinion, leading many to conclude that the Southern code of honorable conduct must not be permitted to disable the cause. By the fall of 1864, in any case, soldiers and leaders on both sides had grown inured to horror, and were quite prepared to contemplate acts from which they would have shrunk three years earlier. It is much harder to say why a thinker as strategic as Benjamin would have seen merit in kidnapping Lincoln. Could he have been exchanged for thousands of soldiers? Perhaps. Would a Lincoln deprived of liberty be amenable to peace terms? Would he have been more amenable if threatened with a trial for capital crimes? Certainly not.

Kidnapping, of course, is not murder. There is, however, a more circumstantial case that Davis and Benjamin approved a plot to kill the president—though not the one ultimately carried out by John Wilkes Booth. One of Booth's confederates, a blockade-runner named George Atzerodt, was arrested soon after the war and gave a confession that was lost for more than a century. Atzerodt said that in early April, Booth had told him that he had just met with "a party" who planned to "mine the end of the pres. house near the War Dept"—the western end of the White House. The goal was to "get the prest. [president] certain."[8]

Booth lacked the know-how for such a plot. However, the War Department maintained a Torpedo Bureau whose job was to manufacture and deploy explosives, including both torpedoes to destroy ships and pressure-triggered land mines to be buried underground. In the last days of March 1865, Thomas Harney, one of the Torpedo Bureau's most seasoned agents, was called to Richmond. John Surratt was present in the city as well, having just returned from Canada with messages for Benjamin and Davis. On April 1, Benjamin submitted two warrants for withdrawals from the "secret service" account that was used only for special operations. At his trial in 1867, Surratt testified that the smaller of the sums, $200, was for him. He insisted that he had conspired with Booth only on the plot to kidnap Lincoln, not to kill him, and added that "we never acquainted [Confederate leaders] with the plan, and they never had anything in the wide world to do with it."[9] The recipient of the larger sum, $1,500, was never identified, though the authors of *Come Retribution* note that Harney was the only other active agent then in Richmond. With the city about to fall, Benjamin may have had some other use for the funds; but as of April 1 he and his colleagues believed that they still had about two weeks before they would have to flee.

That some such plot existed can scarcely be doubted. William H. Snyder, a colleague of Harney's from the Torpedo Bureau, remained behind when Richmond fell to warn Lincoln that a plot had been set in motion within the bureau "aimed at the head of the Yankee government." Lincoln himself "was in great danger." The officer who had received Snyder's statement found it highly credible, and raced to convey it to the president himself. Lincoln listened intently and then murmured, "I cannot bring myself to believe that any human being lives who would do me harm."[10] Harney, meanwhile, traveled north with guerrilla-style units that had continued to wage war even as the armies of the Confederacy were collapsing. On April 8 he reached the Plains, forty-five miles west of Washington. There the forces escorting him were surprised by Union cavalry, and Harney was taken prisoner. He was booked as a member of the Torpedo Bureau, "found with ordnance."[11] But after taking the Oath of Allegiance to the Union, Harney was released, apparently without interrogation.

One cannot easily imagine either Judah Benjamin or Jefferson Davis authorizing the assassination of Abraham Lincoln. In his own words, after all, Benjamin had sternly admonished Lieutenant Capston, his agent in Ireland, to confine himself to means "strictly legitimate, honorable and proper." In any case,

Benjamin and Davis likely would have been checked not only by their deep horror of regicide but by the meager likelihood, by April 1, 1865, that so dreadful an act would seriously alter the course of the war. Nevertheless, in the desperate final months of the Confederacy, military and political leaders were prepared to adopt extreme measures to survive, whether through emancipating slaves or through what we would now call acts of terrorism. Booth's assassination appears to have been carried out with no knowledge and minimal coordination, if any, with leaders in Richmond. The same cannot be said for the efforts that failed, and so faded from history. Those clearly had higher-level support—how much, and how high, we don't know. But history might have judged Judah Benjamin and Jefferson Davis yet more harshly had Thomas Harney made his way to the White House.

By the time Davis's retinue reached Charlotte, Southern zeal had curdled into sullen resignation. Few citizens were prepared to host the Cabinet. Benjamin and Jules were fortunate to find shelter with Abram Weill, one of the city's most prominent Jewish residents. Benjamin thanked his host with a gift of the gold-headed cane he was wont to twirl—a recognition, perhaps, that he would soon have little need of his foppish appurtenances. Long afterward, in 1948, Charlotte returned the favor by erecting a black granite monument on the site of Weill's home commemorating Benjamin's visit. The inscription included thanks from the United Daughters of the Confederacy to "the Jewish community of Charlotte," which paid for the stone. Jewish leaders began agitating in 2017 to have the piece moved. In 2020 the monument was defaced in the midst of Black Lives Matter demonstrations, and was then removed by city officials. As with the passage in *The Plot Against America*, Benjamin's memory survives chiefly as an affront.

General Johnston, commander of the Army of Tennessee, which included virtually all the remaining forces in the Deep South, met with Sherman on April 17 to negotiate terms of surrender. Sherman proved surprisingly magnanimous in victory, offering to receive the Confederate states back into the Union with their governments intact and with no harm to their property—terms that he was in no way authorized to offer. Benjamin concluded that the time had come to stop humoring his mad king. When Davis asked each official to write out his views, Benjamin stated that the terms "were the best and most favorable that we could hope to obtain by a continuance of the struggle." He knew that Davis still dreamed of drawing on new resources in the West; he quashed that hope in writing, "We can obtain no aid from the Trans-Mississippi Department, from which we are cut off by the fleet of gunboats that patrol the river." Davis, he said, should resign. But the president of the Confederacy would never resign. The party pushed farther south, to Abbeville, South Carolina. And when federal authorities revoked the generous terms Sherman had offered, Johnston accepted the harsher ones that Grant had imposed on Lee.[12]

Now Davis's little band of loyalists began to dwindle as men looked to their own future. First the treasury secretary pleaded illness, then the attorney general, then the navy secretary. The generals who had surrendered remained behind. Benjamin stayed by his president's side. Davis continued to talk wildly about the Trans-Mississippi, or about the bold knights who would fight alongside him. "Three thousand brave men," he declared, as if he were Henry V, "are enough for a nucleus around which the whole people will rally when the panic which now afflicts them will pass away." Benjamin did not respond; but the others did, and told Davis that the fight was over. He looked from one to another, and saw his fantasy dashed. "Then all is indeed lost," he said softly, and had to be helped from the room. Still, he

would not resign. Yet again the Confederate government decamped, this time across a rickety pontoon bridge to the little
town of Washington, Georgia.

Here, at last, having concluded that he had satisfied all
imaginable obligations to the great patron of his life, Benjamin
determined to save his own skin. Davis had decided to rejuve-
nate the Confederacy in the remote fastnesses of Texas. Con-
siderate as ever, Benjamin told Davis, as Varina wrote years
later, that "I could not bear the fatigue of riding as you do." He
would instead continue on alone to Florida, though of course
should his help be needed, "I will answer your call at once."
This was mere politesse, as Davis perhaps understood. Benjamin explained to a remaining Cabinet official that he planned
to reach "the farthest place from the United States . . . if it
takes me to the middle of China."[13] He parted from Jules, who
he thought would be safest riding by himself. Jules was later
taken prisoner in Alabama and then released after several weeks,
at which point he returned home to New Orleans.

There soon commenced the greatest of Judah Benjamin's
many acts of impersonation. The group had been joined by
Colonel Henry J. Leovy, an old friend of Benjamin's from New
Orleans, a Jewish lawyer who before the war had owned the
local paper, the *Delta*. Leovy agreed to join Benjamin in a sort
of minstrelsy. Benjamin pretended to be M. M. Bonfals, a traveling Frenchman. Leovy posed as his translator. One of Davis's
aides noted in his diary, "With goggles on, his beard grown, a
hat well over his face, and a large cloak hiding his figure, no
one would have recognized him as the late Secretary of State of
the Confederacy."[14]

The two men wobbled southward in an ambulance on roads
choked with refugees, wounded men, husbandless families, lost
souls, and, of course, freed slaves, their own future as unknow-
able as that of the ruined white people around them. This was
very hard traveling after a month inside the confines of the

floating Confederate government. And it was extremely dangerous; discovery meant almost certain death. In mid-May, Colonel John Taylor Wood, a Davis aide, somehow discovered Benjamin on the road to deliver the news that the president of the
Confederacy had been found and arrested almost as soon as he
had set out for Texas. Benjamin was now the most important
figure still at large among the alleged conspirators in Lincoln's
death.

After several weeks Benjamin discarded his old disguise for
a new one, which so delighted him that once he reached safety
he described his adventures in a letter to his sister Penny. "I
found my most successful disguise to be that of a farmer," he
wrote. "I professed to be travelling in Florida in search of land
on which to settle, with some friends who desired to move
from South Carolina I got a kind farmer's wife to make me some
homespun clothes just like her husband's. I got for my horse
the commonest and roughest equipment I could find."[15] One
can hardly miss the note of mischievous delight. Benjamin enjoyed playing charades, and he enjoyed pulling the wool over
the eyes of his rivals. His enemies had targeted him for death,
but he would outwit them. They thought him a courtroom orator and an effete gourmet but, like the ever-resourceful Ulysses,
he would become whatever he needed to be. Colonel Leovy
found himself moved by this fearless act of shape-shifting. He
would later write, "Traveling in disguise, sleeping at night in
log huts, living on the plainest fare, subjected to all the discom-
forts of such a journey, with all his plans shattered and without
definite hope for the future, his superb confidence and courage
raised him above all."[16]

Benjamin parted from Leovy, who returned to New Orleans, and headed west in the hope of finding a boat to take him
down the coast, traveling at night and resting during the day.
He later told a story that while he hid in a thicket he was startled by a voice: "Hi, for Jeff." A parrot—obviously a Confeder-

ate parrot—was jabbering away in the branches above his head. Benjamin threw a stone at the bird, and then followed its path as it flew to what Benjamin hoped would be its owner's home. There Benjamin did, indeed, find Confederate sympathizers prepared to shelter and feed him, and to sew his heavy store of gold securely into his vest and waistband. This so resembles a passage from *The Odyssey* or some other work of legend that one can only say that it was the tale Benjamin later chose to tell.[17]

Benjamin finally reached the Gulf of Mexico, where he found a former Confederate officer, Captain Tresca, who agreed to take him six hundred miles down the coast in his open boat. Another man served as mate. Benjamin parted with $1,500 in gold. For more than two weeks, starting June 23, the three sat exposed to blazing heat and occasional storms, subsisting on turtle eggs and fish, acutely aware that any moment they could encounter a Union gunboat. And so they did. At that point, Captain Tresca ordered Benjamin to go down in the galley, cover himself with grease, and present himself as the cook. Nothing, of course, could have been more congenial to this master of disguise. The imposture worked so well that one of the officers remarked that he had never before seen a Jew doing manual labor.[18]

With the Caribbean island of Bimini almost in sight on a hot, windless evening, the horizon turned black with storm, and then Benjamin and his companions saw that they were surrounded by "water-spouts"—tornadoes at sea, which appeared to be solid pillars of water. "At about nine o'clock," Benjamin wrote in the letter to Penny, "a very heavy, lurid cloud dipped down towards the sea, and in a single minute two large water-spouts were formed, and the wind began blowing furiously directly toward us, bringing the water-spouts in a straight line for the boat. . . . The furious whirl of the water could be distinctly heard, as in a long wavering column that swayed about in the breeze and extended from the ocean up into the cloud, the spouts advanced in their course." The storm hit the rickety craft before the tornadoes did, so that the rain and wind seemed likely to sink them before the waterspouts could. Meanwhile, a new waterspout had formed behind them. The first two columns passed a hundred yards from the ship, "tearing up the whole surface of the sea as they passed, and whirling it furiously into the clouds, with a roar such as is heard at the foot of Niagara Falls." Those columns raced into the one behind them, which "wavered and broke," Benjamin wrote. Fifteen minutes later, "all was calm and still," and on July 10 they put in to Bimini.

Benjamin hoped to catch a ship to one of the main English islands and thence to Southampton. The destination Benjamin had set for himself throughout this epic journey was England, for he had had the foresight to send ahead to Liverpool six or seven hundred bales of cotton that he could redeem for cash once he arrived. But he was destined to endure still more perils before reaching safety. The cargo of the ship he boarded in Bimini was jammed tight with sponges that quickly dried, hardened, and split the hold. Benjamin described the ordeal in his letter to Penny:

> We left Bemini on Thursday afternoon, the 13th, and on Friday morning about half-past seven o'clock, the ship foundered at sea, thirty miles from the nearest land, sinking with such rapidity that we had barely time to jump into a small skiff that the sloop had in tow before she went to the bottom.
>
> In the skiff, leaky, but with a single oar, with no provisions save a pot of rice that had just been cooked for breakfast, and a small keg of water, I found myself at eight o'clock in the morning, with three negroes for my companions in disaster, only five inches of the boat out of water, on the broad ocean, with the certainty that we could not survive five minutes if the sea became the least rough. We started, however, quite courageously for the land, and without any signs of trepidation from anyone on board and the weather con-

tinuing very calm, we proceeded landward till about eleven
o'clock, when a vessel was discerned in the distance, which
was supposed to be a small schooner, and which we felt sure
of reaching if the weather continued calm.

The friendly ship's captain returned Benjamin and his mates
to Bimini. It is notable that Benjamin praises the imperturb-
ability of his crew members but says nothing about himself. He
appears to have been, as usual, unfazed in the moment of disaster. Benjamin would later write his friend Thomas Bayard that,
despite weeks in an open boat, "exposed to the tropical sun in
June and July, utterly without shelter or a change of clothes,"
he had never had "one minute's indisposition nor despondency
but was rather pleased by the feeling of triumph in disappoint-
ing the malice of my enemies."[19] Nor had he failed to keep
his loved ones in mind. He mentioned to his sister that while
"passing through Georgia" he had left $900 in gold, "all that I
could spare," to be delivered to "Sis and Hatty in LaGrange"—
the town in Georgia to which they had moved after Louisiana
fell to the Yankees in 1862.

The wreck off the coast of Bimini did not even mark the
end of Benjamin's misadventures. He chartered a sloop to take
him to Nassau, one hundred miles distant, but, he wrote to
Penny, "we were so baffled by calms, squalls, and head winds,
that we were six days making it." In Nassau he met a distant
relation, Alexander Benjamin, who took him in and provided
for all his wants. He had, he said, read that Jefferson Davis was
being tortured in prison, perhaps in the hopes of killing him
rather than bringing him to trial. (In fact Davis was indicted for
treason and allowed to remain free while the proceedings dragged
on; later he was included in the general amnesty issued by President Andrew Johnson on Christmas Day 1868.) Benjamin left
no doubt about his reverence for the Confederate leader: "No
nobler gentleman, no purer man, no more exalted patriot ever

drew breath; and eternal infamy will blacken the base and savage wretches who are now taking advantage of their brief grasp of power to wreak a cowardly vengeance on his honored head."

From Nassau, Benjamin took a schooner to Havana, and then another ship to St. Thomas, of which he retained only the very dimmest memories from his infancy. There he finally caught a steamer to England. Fate seemed determined to sound the very depths of Benjamin's talents for survival: At about nine in the evening on the first night at sea, a fire began raging in the ship's hold. "By dint of great exertion and admirable conduct and discipline exhibited by all on board," Benjamin wrote to Penny, "the flames were kept from bursting through the deck till we got back to the harbor of St. Thomas, where we arrived at about three o'clock in the morning with seven feet of water in the hold poured in by the steam pumps, and the deck burned to within an eighth of an inch of its entire thickness." Remarkably, crews in port were able to ready the ship to sail again in three days. At last Benjamin's luck held: the steamer reached Southampton on August 30. He was virtually penniless, just as he had been when he arrived in New Orleans almost forty years earlier. As he had there, he would once again hoist himself to the highest station in an adopted land.

6

London

AFTER A WEEK in London, Benjamin crossed the Channel and was reunited with his family in Paris. Not since Ninette was a baby more than thirty years earlier had they lived together, save for brief visits. Banishment from America had at long last made that possible.

John Slidell, who had remained in Paris, promised to introduce Benjamin to bankers who could set him up in comfort. But Benjamin declined; he had determined to return to London to pursue a new career as a barrister. We hardly need wonder at the decision, since Natalie had brought him little beyond pain and humiliation. In Paris she lived well; in London she would have to share his privations, which was wholly contrary to her nature. The only surviving scrap of correspondence from Natalie to her husband, from the 1850s, reads, "Oh, talk not to me of economy! It is so fatiguing."[1] In a letter to Penny, Benjamin did not even mention his wife, though he reported that Ninette was "as blooming as a rose."[2]

For a Southern gentleman, even one marinated in the rich *jus* of the Vieux Carré, London constituted the very last word in gentility. And for one of America's great lawyers, no title could have been more gratifying than "British barrister." As he wrote to Penny, "Nothing is more independent, nor offers a more promising future, than admission as a barrister to the bar of London." Benjamin would have to spend three years as an apprentice at Lincoln's Inn; that was the rule. Three years was a very long time for an almost destitute fifty-four-year-old. But Benjamin returned to London and enrolled himself. He made ends meet by writing unsigned "leaders," or editorials, for the *Daily Telegraph*, at five pounds a week. He had high hopes for the six hundred bales of cotton he had sent ahead, but only a hundred of them made it to Liverpool. Prices remained stratospheric in the aftermath of the war, and Benjamin cleared $20,000 from the sale. His money woes, at least, appeared to be solved; but in early 1866, Overend, Gurney & Company, the British firm in which he had deposited most of his funds, went bankrupt, carrying his money with it.

Benjamin had apparently reached Europe with small amounts of gold remaining from his journey; this he doled out to Natalie in Paris, who lived vastly more comfortably than he did but apparently did not feel any scruples about the continuation of her subsidies. The former secretary of state of the Confederacy lived much as he had as a clerk in his first years in New Orleans, dining on bread and cheese in cheap restaurants where there was little danger of running into an acquaintance. In a letter to his former law partner, E. A. Bradford, he listed the expenses associated with the Inns of Court: "Stamps 25 pounds . . . Lectures 5 pounds . . . Admission fees 5 pounds . . . Printed forms 11 pounds . . ." He told Bradford that he could make a decent living as the sub-editor of a newspaper; but that would interfere with his legal studies. The cheese-paring was worth it.

Benjamin was amused rather than ashamed by his new sta-

tus in the lowliest depths of the legal pecking order; he knew
that his gifts would ultimately land him in the station he deserved. Dining at Lincoln's Inn was required, and he described
to Bradford the hierarchy of the occasion: "Benchers," the most
senior figures of the bar, at the head table; then forty or fifty
barristers; and finally "the students to the number of about 150
including your humble servant, all seated at long tables and
dressed in stuff gowns, which the waiters throw over us in the
ante-chamber before we enter the dining hall." The waiter
would deposit the dishes among groups of four, with each man
helping himself rather than serving one another. That didn't
seem genteel at all, yet Benjamin loved the freedom of conversation. "One dines almost every day with some stranger, but
the rule is that all are presumed to be gentlemen and conversation is at once established with entire abandon, as if the parties
were old acquaintances."[3]

Benjamin enjoyed a social status wholly at variance with his
economic position. He seems to have suffered no ill treatment
as a Jew, despite the pervasive anti-Semitism of Britain's upper
classes. The other great Benjamin of the day, Disraeli, then led
the Tory party, though he had converted to the Anglican Church.
The situation might have been different had Judah Benjamin
sought to lay claims to a position of rank, as Disraeli had; but
he was a political refugee who had, in effect, thrown himself
upon the mercy of his hosts. Nor was he despised as a former
slaveholder and pillar of the Confederacy. Only the radicals
would have raised so indelicate a matter. Gentlemen treated
Benjamin as a person of consequence. He dined with William
Gladstone, leader of the Liberal party, chancellor of the Exchequer, and soon to be prime minister; Gladstone had been highly
sympathetic to the Confederacy, and thus regarded Benjamin
more as a dispossessed national leader than as the defender of a
reprehensible cause.

Benjamin had always moved easily in polite society; his gifts of manner and of conversation could not fail to please in this most polite of all societies. Invited to spend a weekend at the country seat of Baron Pollock, the father of the barrister with whom he trained, Benjamin found himself very much in his element: "in the midst of the proverbial splendor of an English gentleman's country seat, and with a crowd of titled and fashionable guests, I found their tone, manners and customs just what I expected—quiet, easy, courteous, and agreeable. The style, of course, exceeds anything seen on our side of the water."[4] Here was the real thing of which American society remained the pale copy.

Benjamin was, of course, no ordinary law student. Charles Pollock asked Benjamin to take a look at a request he had received from the Metropolitan Police asking what rights they had to search prisoners for evidence of crimes prior to trial. Pollock later described his amazement at the results: "Benjamin took the papers and at once set to work to consider the authorities and deal with the questions with such purpose that when I returned from court they were all disposed of. The only fault that could be found was that the learning was too great for the occasion, going back to first principles in justification of each answer."[5]

Even the British bar, with its regard for tradition, recognized the absurdity of requiring so self-evidently competent a figure to waste three years dining in Lincoln's Inn. Benjamin's nationality might have posed an obstacle, but in his petition for admission to the bar he described himself as a "political exile" who had been born to British parents in British territory and thus qualified as a dual citizen. Senior benchers of Lincoln's Inn joined the petition, and Benjamin was called to the bar on June 6, 1866, only six months after he had enrolled. While he had to continue mastering the fine points of English law, Benjamin's vast experience with American cases and case law, and his gift for organizing in his head an immense body of fact, made him an expert advocate even as a very junior figure. The first piece of legal work he did for Pollock as a barrister required him to write a new set of underwriting principles for a ship insurance firm in only forty-eight hours. The two more experienced barristers Pollock approached had already begged off, pleading the shortage of time. Benjamin had made a very steady living off ship insurance a generation earlier. "His own knowledge of the requirements told him what was wanting," Pollock wrote; "and the very next morning, commencing after an early breakfast, and never pausing for a mid-day meal, he worked on steadily, and shortly before eight, the hour at which he usually dined, the rules were complete, written out in his own neat hand . . . with scarcely an alteration from beginning to end, as if he had been composing a poem."[6]

Pollock quickly came to recognize that Benjamin's experience gave him some advantages even over leading members of the British bar. He had trained in Louisiana, which used the Justinian Code that later became the foundation of European law. "The principles and practice of this great system of law Benjamin knew and appreciated thoroughly," Pollock wrote, "and he was at all times ready to point out its leading features, and how they differed in principle from English law. This also gave him a distinct position superior to his brother advocates, when arguing, before the judicial committee of our privy council, appeals from the English colonies of French origin which were ceded to England before the code." Moreover, he added, "Few men had a sounder or wider range of knowledge and experience of the law-merchant, including shipping, insurance, and foreign trading than Benjamin."[7]

Within a few years Benjamin had gained real standing in the British bar. And he knew his own worth very well. Once he was asked to examine a set of legal documents for a fee of five guineas. (A guinea was worth five cents more than a pound.) He left them untouched. When the firm in question sent a clerk to pick up the work, Benjamin explained that "the fee covered taking the papers, but not examining them." The fee was promptly increased to twenty-five guineas. Nevertheless, Benjamin found work only slowly, and often had time on his hands. In 1867 he hit on the idea of repeating the success he had had as a young attorney with his digest of Louisiana law. A new book he had begun working on, he told Penny, "will bring me into more prominence in the profession and perhaps secure a more rapid advance in getting business."[8] *Benjamin's Treatise on the Law of Sale of Personal Property: With Reference to the American Decisions and the French Code of Civil Law*—known to ensuing generations of law students, lawyers, and judges as *Benjamin on Sales*—appeared in August 1868, two years after Benjamin had been called to the bar. It seems scarcely credible that one man could have written so definitive a tract, running to over a thousand pages, in little over a year, while simultaneously earning a living as a lawyer. One is reminded of Samuel Johnson's quip when asked how he could possibly write his famous dictionary in three years when it had taken forty Frenchmen forty years to create theirs: "As three to sixteen hundred, so is the proportion of an Englishman to a Frenchman."[9] The ratio was perhaps a bit more modest in Benjamin's case (and Johnson actually required nine years to finish the job).

Benjamin on Sales, by far the most important work by a man who consciously chose a life of action rather than reflection, is a vast compendium, covering not only the nature of contract and its legal ramifications, but the difference among legal traditions—the English, the French, the American, as well as the Scottish and others. At the end of each section Benjamin appended an American note. To take only a single example in order to convey the immensity of the enterprise, at the end of Book 1, "The Formation of the Contract," Benjamin observes that under American law a sale is to be distinguished from, among others, "a Contract to sell in future," the posting of bail, a consignment, an act of barter, and so on. Benjamin illustrates each of the eight exceptions he cites with dozens of cases. As a separate matter, he addresses the vexed question of "the delivery of liquor by a club to its members." On this issue alone, Benjamin cites dozens of cases. And so on through "What is a sufficient Note of the Bargain made," "Personal Actions against the Buyer when Property has not passed," "Sale of Chattel not Specific"—no indelicate reference to slavery included.[10]

Benjamin on Sales quickly came to be seen as indispensable. Not long after publication, Baron Samuel Martin, a judge, asked his clerk to produce a copy. "Never heard of it," said the clerk. "Never heard of it!" the Baron spluttered. "Mind that I never take my seat here again without that book at my side."[11] Only twice in his career—and thirty-five years apart—did Benjamin turn his hand to a work of legal scholarship: the first proved invaluable in Louisiana, the second in England.

Nevertheless, the barriers to a successful career turned out to be higher than they had been in New Orleans, where everything was possible for a man of merit. In a letter to his older sister Rebecca in early 1870, Benjamin admitted, "I had anticipated from the growth of my reputation at the bar here and from the assurances of those who ought to know, that I would already have been in receipt of an income sufficient for support at all events." In fact, he wrote, "the attorneys give their briefs whenever they possibly can, to barristers who are connected or related in some way with them or with their families; and in an old country like England, these family ties are so ramified that there is hardly an attorney who has not a barrister whom it is his interest to engage." He would always be the outsider; he would always have to work harder, and shine more brilliantly, in order to succeed as others did. Nevertheless, he was in the harness, where he was happiest, and he had put far behind him the crowds of crippled men, the famished civilians, the anti-Semitic gibes, the fear of capture and death that had shadowed his life for four long years. "I work hard," he wrote, "but it is a happy life for me to be absorbed in my studies and business, and to have no harassing anxieties to disturb my labors."[12]

It is easy to regard Benjamin's abrupt departure from Jefferson Davis as the self-serving act of the natural-born survivor. Yet Benjamin seemed to feel the tribulations of the Confederate president and his wife almost as keenly as he did those of his own family. The day after he reached London from Southampton he wrote Varina a long letter informing her that he had instructed a Confederate business agent in London to place $12,500, Davis's salary up through June 30, in an account for her. He sought to relieve her of any sense of guilt she might feel about drawing on it: "you are indebted for it to no individual and are under no obligations to anyone for it. . . I beg however that you will not apply any of it towards the personal use of Mr. Davis or any expenses of his trial of defence; for I know, I am absolutely certain, that a very large sum, five times as much as will probably be wanted, is already placed in perfectly safe hands, to be used solely for his service."

Benjamin's feelings for both Varina and her husband are obviously sincere, yet the letter is also suffused with a note of penitence. He had left Davis in Georgia, "charged by him to perform certain public duties in Nassau and Havana, and then to rejoin him in Texas." Benjamin had never intended to fulfill the last part of that promise, and of course he hadn't. Why hadn't he reacted to news of Davis's capture? "God knows what I have suffered since my first reception of the horrible news that my beloved and honored friend was in the hands of the enemy," Benjamin wrote, perhaps laying it on a bit thick. He described his weeks in the marshes of Florida, his passage toward the Florida Keys, the shipwreck in the Gulf, the trip to England. Now he was at last safe—but very far from Texas. In closing, he asked, "Can I, my dear friend, do anything, in any way, by any sacrifice, to aid you or Mr. Davis in this dreadful crisis? If so, command me without scruple."[13]

Benjamin found an opportunity to demonstrate his loyalty to Davis with no danger to himself when Davis was charged with violating the laws of war by cruel treatment of Union prisoners, a charge added to an earlier one of complicity in the assassination of Lincoln. This was a very grave allegation; later that year Captain Henry Wirz, former commander of the Confederate prison at Andersonville, Georgia, was found guilty of abusing prisoners, and hanged. Benjamin sent a long letter to the *Sunday Times*, which the *New York Times* reprinted on September 25, 1865. It was the North, not the South, he wrote, that had refused exchanges of prisoners, a "policy which consigned hundreds of thousands of wretched men to captivity apparently hopeless." The South, with its perpetual manpower shortage, needed prisoner exchanges far more than did the North. Lincoln's refusal to exchange all but the most enfeebled prisoners, Benjamin asserted, "contributed to our overthrow more, perhaps, than any other single measure."[14]

Benjamin would have known that as Davis's hated chief aide he could have virtually no influence on American public opinion. At the very least, though, he could signal to Varina, to Davis, and to his former colleagues in the Cabinet, all of them in federal captivity save the former secretary of war John C. Breckinridge, that his flight to Europe did not mean a slackening of fidelity to the cause. Of Davis himself he wrote, "I have learned to know him better, perhaps than he is known by any living man. Neither in private conversation nor in cabinet council have I ever heard him utter one unworthy thought, one ungenerous sentiment." In saying so, Benjamin was, of course, clearing his own name as much as that of Davis.

In May 1866, the government reduced the charge of complicity in Lincoln's assassination to one of treason, and added the names of others, including Robert E. Lee and Benjamin himself. Whatever hopes Benjamin might have had of being able to visit the United States in the near future were now dashed; he would be arrested the moment he stepped off a steamer.

Benjamin might not have been a great deal more popular in the South than he was in the North. The men who had hated him during the war, and who had been happy to use him as a scapegoat for the failures of the Confederacy, hated him all the more now that he had escaped to safety, thus confirming their view that his only real concern was for himself. Henry S. Foote, the former governor of Mississippi and member of the Confederate Congress, alleged that Benjamin—and Davis—had always planned to escape to England, where they had secreted Confederate gold.[15] Benjamin was regularly accused of stealing some of the gold that had gone missing in the chaotic last days of the war—not the several thousand dollars' worth that he may have availed himself of, but millions.

In 1866 another of his inveterate enemies, former Confederate senator Louis Wigfall of Texas, reported to a friend from London that Benjamin "has turned out to be an Englishman & as he has plenty of money & can attend the clubs, entertain friends & extend his acquaintance he found no difficulty in being admitted after six months at the Inns. . . . On his arrival here he reported himself authorized by the president to take charge of financial matters & my own belief is that he and the agents have divided among themselves all that is left of Confederate funds."[16] The clear implication of "turned out to be an Englishman" is that Benjamin had never truly been a Southerner.

In fact, Benjamin never ceased to be a Southerner. He appears never to have changed his views of the merits of the war, any more than other leaders of the Lost Cause did. In a letter to Thomas Bayard in November 1865, Benjamin argued that "if the Southern states are allowed without interference to regulate the transition of the negro from his former state to that of a freed man they will eventually work out the problem successfully. . . . But if they are obstructed and thwarted by the fanatics, and if external influences are brought to bear on the negro and influence his ignorant fancy with wild dreams of social and political equality, I shudder for the bitter future which is in store for my unhappy country."[17] In short, the South must remain free to govern itself as it sees fit, including by treating former slaves as lesser humans and second-class citizens. This was, of course, precisely the view that Benjamin had expressed when he advocated the emancipation of slaves in order to swell the ranks of the Confederate army.

Yet Wigfall was also right. Benjamin had an extraordinary gift for adapting to new surroundings, for facing forward no matter what lay behind him. In the fall of 1868, during one of the many intervals of his interminable trial, Jefferson Davis came to England along with Varina. Citing a pressing legal engagement, Benjamin did not come to Liverpool to greet the Davises as they disembarked. However, they soon met in London. Varina had spent the previous three years with the acolytes of the Lost Cause, endlessly re-litigating the past. She was startled to observe that her old friend "appeared happier than I had ever seen him." Although "he gave Mr. Davis one long talk about Confederate matters," she noted, "after that he seemed averse to speaking of them. . . . In speaking of his grief over our defeat, he said that the power of dismissing any painful memory had served him well after the fall of the Confederacy."[18] When Davis asked Benjamin how he should respond to a libelous book-length attack, his old counselor advised him to preserve his silence, and thus his peace of mind.

Within three or four years of gaining admission to the bar, Benjamin had achieved in England something like the professional status he had enjoyed in Louisiana. He had a bravura manner that might have offended lawyers and judges had his mastery of facts, law, and argument not been so self-evident. In

1869 he was called on to defend Colin McRae, the Confederate agent in London—the figure with whom Louis Wigfall had accused him of conspiring. The United States government was seeking to seize funds held by the Confederacy, including from loans that Benjamin himself had negotiated.

Benjamin and his colleagues faced some of England's greatest lawyers, including a future lord chancellor. When it became clear that the judge, Vice Chancellor William Milbourne James, had accepted the merits of the plaintiff's case, Benjamin leaped to his feet and said, to the astonishment of all present, "if you will only listen to me"—and then repeated this phrase twice more in an increasingly urgent crescendo—"I pledge myself you will dismiss this suit with costs"—that is, that he would require the plaintiff to pay the defendant's legal expenses. Benjamin then spoke without pause for "an hour or two," according to a court reporter, and as he did so the courtroom filled with onlookers who had heard the news of this remarkable performance. At the end, precisely as Benjamin had predicted, the judges dismissed the case with costs.[19]

In 1870 Benjamin argued his first case before the House of Lords. Within a few years he was appearing almost only before the Lords or the Privy Council, a tribunal consisting of Cabinet ministers and other high officials that heard the most consequential cases from across the Empire. Benjamin aspired to be named Queen's Counsel, an honorific conferred by the monarch. Though he was never granted this title, in 1872, thanks to the intercession of senior judges, he was given a "patent of precedence" that ranked him above all future Queen's Counsels. This was an unprecedented honor for an American lawyer, not to mention one who had been practicing in England for only six years.

In a letter to his sisters, Benjamin affected to make light of the achievement, reporting that "I have now to wear a full-bottomed wig, with wings falling down my shoulders and knee breeches

and black silk stockings and shoes with buckles and in this ri-
diculous array, in my silk gown, to present myself at the next
levee to Her Majesty to return thanks for her gracious kindness." He sent a photograph of himself in all his glory, implor-
ing the family to keep the glamorous details to themselves while
at the same time bruiting about the fact of his promotion in
New Orleans.

Benjamin's period of struggle in England was now over. He
had risen to the top, as he had risen to the top in every prior
episode of his life. In Richmond, his status had depended on
a patron who protected him from innumerable enemies; now
he was fully self-reliant, as he always wished to be. And he had
no enemies. By 1871 his income had reached 2,100 pounds, or
$10,500. Two years later—after his patent of precedence—the
figure had quadrupled. In 1876 he earned almost 14,000 pounds.
An article in the *New York Times* in 1879 put his annual income,
including fees, investment, and royalties from *Benjamin on Sales*,
then in its third printing, at $150,000—a bit under $4 million
in today's terms.[20] As ever, he lavished very little on himself.
In 1873, he took rooms in a house in Ryder Street, a charming
bow-shaped lane in the very elegant neighborhood of St. James,
and six years later moved around the corner to Duke Street.
But he neither bought nor built a residence for himself.

Benjamin managed to recreate the patrician life he had first
forged years earlier in New Orleans. Though he typically worked
at night and thus socialized little, he often dined with friends at
his club, the Junior Athenaeum, which had opened its doors
only in 1864 and welcomed members of Parliament, fellows of
the learned societies, men of literature and the arts. Benjamin
kept clear of British politics, but he remained a Tory at heart.
In the mid-1860s, the House of Commons was convulsed with
the Reform Bill advanced by the Liberal government of Lord
Palmerston, and then of Earl Russell. (This is the subject of
Anthony Trollope's great novel *Phineas Finn*.) The bill signifi-

cantly expanded the franchise among urban working-class men. Though now living in perhaps the greatest city in the world, Benjamin regarded industrial democracy with the profound skepticism of the antebellum plantation owner. In a letter to his friend Bayard in 1871, he wrote, "I quite share your opinion that stable government by the people is absolutely impossible in countries where the urban population have a preponderance in political affairs, and I cannot doubt that democratic institutions will still linger in Western America long after in the more populous East they will have been replaced by some other form of government as the sole refuge from absolute anarchy." He accused the "Manchester Cotton School"—England's free-market liberals, then ascendant—of surrendering national politics to the mob. A decade later, he would write succinctly, "Nothing is so abhorrent to me as the Radicalism which seeks to elevate the population into the governing class."[21]

Benjamin appeared to be every inch an English gentleman, and not just to envious visitors like Louis Wigfall but to the English themselves, who had showered him with legal honors. Yet his position was more precarious than it looked. Joseph G. Witt, his executor, later wrote that Benjamin "was compelled to work late in the evening, and that was a necessity against which his whole soul revolted. But his determination to make money not for himself . . . but for those he loved conquered his aversion."[22] Though he may have been squirreling away some of that money for his own retirement, Benjamin did, in fact, assume very large obligations to his family. He continued to support his sisters in New Orleans. He lost $25,000 he had invested with his brother, Joseph. He regularly sent funds to Natalie and Ninette.

In 1874, at the very advanced age of thirty, Ninette married Henri de Bousignac, a captain in the French army. It was a very gratifying match for Benjamin, and presumably for his wife as well. "He is of excellent family," Benjamin wrote, "irreproachable habits, beloved by all around him for his frank, gay, and amiable character." Benjamin worried that Ninette, who may have inherited her mother's habits, would not manage to get by on a soldier's salary. "By giving up all my savings," he wrote, "I have been able to settle on Ninette three thousand dollars a year, so that her future is now secure against want."[23]

Benjamin appeared to be almost the only self-sufficient person in his family; it fell to him to care for the others. Jules St. Martin came from New Orleans for his niece's wedding and then remained in Paris, staying with the Benjamins. He seems never to have made anything of himself, and to have remained an elegant and charming family dependent. Now he was gravely ill. "I am depressed in spirits on account of the condition of poor Jules," Benjamin wrote his sister. Jules had gone to the south of France for the winter; but he died the following year. This must have been a devastating loss to Benjamin, and perhaps to Natalie as well, for Captain de Bousignac had been transferred from Versailles to Orléans, and Ninette had gone with him. Natalie was now alone, and, nearing sixty, she could hardly count on the allure she had once enjoyed.

Benjamin's yearning to visit his family in New Orleans shines through his letters home; he doted on his sisters' children, sending them stamps for which he hunted through the shops of Paris even when they were too old to care about them. But he never did return. Besides the expense, which he felt he could not afford, he could not know what kind of reception he would receive even in the South. However, he put the blame on the gross injustice, as he saw it, of Reconstruction. In 1875 he wrote to Rebecca, "You say, my dearest, that I never speak of visiting you at all. I never *can* consent to go to New Orleans and break my heart with witnessing the rule of negroes and carpet-baggers. I have hoped year by year that some change would be effected which would place decent and respectable men at the head of the administration of affairs, and it seems to me that the time is now fast approaching. I long and yearn to press you all to my heart once again, and for some of us at least age is creeping on and not much time is to be lost."[24] He was sixty-four years old.

Benjamin had achieved extraordinary success by dint of staggering labor; he later told a correspondent that he had worked longer hours as a barrister in London than he had as a member of Jefferson Davis's Cabinet. The time finally came when he felt that he could ease off the throttle. In 1877 he wrote home, "I very seldom have to work after seven in the evening, and from ten in the morning to seven in the evening is no excess of labor!" Two years later he had relaxed his grip further still: "I am beginning again to go into society, which I had relinquished for years, and to accept invitations to dinner which I had habitually declined."[25] In 1881 he went so far as to spend the summer with his family at a spa in the Pyrénées and at the beach in Biarritz.

The one extravagant temptation that Benjamin could never resist was the feathering of splendid nests, at least so long as they included his luxury-loving wife. He had decided that he would spend his last years in Paris with his family. In 1879 Benjamin began building a mansion at 41, Avenue d'Iéna in Paris. Iéna was one of the grand boulevards imposed on the ancient map of Paris in Baron Haussmann's modernization campaign of the 1860s. The city's mercantile new rich flocked to these sparkling precincts. Benjamin himself had always been partial to aristocratic districts, whether the French Quarter or St. James; one could easily imagine him moving into an *hôtel particulier* in one of the city's ancient *faubourgs*. Perhaps the Avenue d'Iéna was a concession to Natalie's gaudier tastes. Whatever the case, Benjamin lavished his wealth on the project—$80,000, he wrote in a letter to Penny. The house no longer stands, but one can see its like up and down the block—three-story limestone structures with massive front doors, carved balcony and balustrades, fine scrollwork above the windows.

If nothing else, the house offered a project for the idle hands of Natalie and Ninette. In a letter home, Benjamin described them as "busy as bees, finishing the furnishing and ornamentation of the 'grand salon,' and threatening to give several soirées during the winter on the pretext that they want to establish intimate relations with certain grand personages who can aid in the rapid promotion of the Captain."[26] It must have been a very grand house, indeed. Benjamin had finally given Natalie exactly what she wanted.

Benjamin had planned to retire to Paris once his home was finished, but he continued to beaver away at his profession in London, whether out of long habit or concern about finances. Visitors found him still flourishing. In 1879 a reporter from the *New York Times*, after spending time with Benjamin in his chambers at the Lambs Building in the Middle Temple, wrote, "Very seldom, indeed, does one meet a man who, having almost attained the scriptural threescore and ten, looks and acts like a man of forty."[27] He had somehow managed to get through an extremely eventful life without serious injury. Then, in May 1880, this jaunty old gentleman jumped off a tram car in Paris while it was still moving rapidly—and was thrown violently to the ground. "My right arm was torn from the socket," he told his friend Bayard, "the shoulder blade broken, and the left side of the forehead fractured." Only his hat, he said, had preserved him from death.[28]

Benjamin never fully recovered from what he called "the shock given to my whole system." By the fall of 1882 he was writing from Paris that he could preserve his health only by resting quietly. "I have been hard at work since I was ten years old," he wrote, "and now I am 72, and have fairly earned some repose."[29] (In fact he was seventy-one.) In February 1883 he wrote to his sister to say that he had been suffering from difficulty breathing, swollen feet, and a chronic exhaustion that had made it difficult even to walk. Doctors in Paris had diagnosed heart failure and imposed a regimen of complete rest. He had announced his retirement from the bar and, it was reported, returned $100,000 in retainers. To his astonishment, he wrote, "Every leading newspaper, with the *Times* at the head, has made my retirement a matter of national concern and regret and my table is covered with piles of letters (some sixty or seventy at least) from my brethren of the bar, expressing the warmest sympathy and regret." Despite his pretense of humility, he added that he had been the subject of testimonials of character *"such as no member of the English bar has ever received."*[30] He must have found these letters an inexpressibly sweet rebuttal to the aspersions attached to his name in the country he had once called home.

More flattering still, Benjamin received a letter from Attorney General Henry James stating that the leading members of the English bar had signed a statement asking him to hold a public farewell dinner for Benjamin, an honor that Benjamin described as unprecedented. On June 30, 1883, the flower of British legal practice convened in the great wood-paneled hall of the Middle Temple. Benjamin sat at the dais along with the attorney general and Lord Selborne, the lord chancellor. In his toast, Sir Henry said, "We found a place for him in our foremost rank; we grudged him not the leadership he so easily gained— we were proud of his success, for we knew the strength of the stranger among us and the bar is ever generous even in its rivalry toward success that is based on merit." That, of course, is what Benjamin had most sought for himself in life—a welcome based only on merit. Benjamin said as much in his response: "I never had an occasion to feel that anyone regarded me as an intruder. I never felt a touch of professional jealousy. I never received an unkindness."[31] This appears to have been quite literally true.

Benjamin then returned to Paris to enjoy what he hoped would be a suitably elegant and dignified retirement. There he received a visit from Francis Lawley, a former member of Parliament, a rake who had gambled away his inheritance, fled to the United States, and begun writing for the *Times*. He had come to know Benjamin while covering the Civil War and had resumed the friendship when he returned to England. Lawley considered Benjamin a great man. For years he had pressed his friend to write his memoirs. Only when Benjamin flatly refused did Lawley ask permission to write an authorized biography. He came to Paris to renew the request. It was then, as Lawley revealed in the introductory chapter of the book that he never completed, that Benjamin told him that he had kept no documents and wished no record to be made of his life. He would, he said, be happy to help prepare a digest of his legal career in England; nothing else. The one precious gift that Lawley left to future historians was the long letter that he solicited from Varina Davis in 1898. Absent that, we would know little of Benjamin's intimate relationship with Jefferson Davis, the great patron of his life. Varina may have loved Benjamin; certainly she looked back across the wreck of years with the sweetness and the sympathy of love.

In April 1884, Benjamin wrote to Lawley to say that he had been ill, confined to "my bed and my arm-chair," but that he believed he had "turned the corner."[32] It was not so. Benjamin died on May 6. In a final act of utter self-absorption, Natalie summoned a Catholic priest, who administered last rites to a man who, though indifferent to his own Jewish faith, had never abandoned it. She also arranged a Catholic funeral service. He was buried alongside the Bousignac family in Père Lachaise, the cemetery of celebrities and *grands bourgeois* in the 20th arrondissement of Paris. Benjamin lies beneath an oblong slab that is scarcely noticeable in the forest of neoclassical mortuary temples and plinths. Natalie had him listed as "Philippe Benjamin," the name that she—and only she—insisted on using. Benjamin had thus been assimilated to Christianity at last by *force majeure*.

Would a just God have denied Benjamin the wealth, the honors, the ease, the self-satisfaction that he enjoyed for the last twenty years of his life? He had, after all, served as an indispensable cog in an evil machine. That he sincerely believed in that machine hardly palliates our judgment, any more than the fact that he believed in the plantation economy from which he benefited.

We cannot regard his role in the slave system as a mere foible, as his earlier biographers did. Yet Benjamin had greatness in him. That greatness lies less in his brilliance, which naturally elevated him among others, than in his pluck, his resilience in the face of catastrophe, his readiness to start over again and again. He is the man whose mild Havana cigar made a tiny point of light in the wild darkness of flight, as his carriage lay stuck in the mud, and a voice like a silver bell rang out with the verses of "Ode on the Death of the Duke of Wellington":

> Where shall we lay the man whom we deplore?
> . . .
> Let the sound of those he wrought for
> And the feet of those he fought for,
> Echo round his bones for evermore.

Introduction

1. Eli N. Evans, *Judah P. Benjamin, the Jewish Confederate* (New York: Free Press, 1988), 38.

2. Varina Davis, letter to Francis Lawley, in Lawley Mss.

3. Stephen Vincent Benét, *John Brown's Body* (New York: Doubleday, Doran, 1928), verse 68.

4. Francis Lawley, biographical manuscript, in Lawley Mss.

5. Philip Roth, *The Plot Against America* (Boston: Houghton Mifflin, 2004), 104–5.

6. Evans, *Judah P. Benjamin*, 9.

7. Robert Douthat Meade, *Judah P. Benjamin: Confederate Statesman* (New York: Oxford University Press, 1943), 378.

Chapter 1. Charleston

1. Bertram Korn, *Eventful Years and Experiences: Studies in Nineteenth Century Jewish History* (Cincinnati: American Jewish Archives, 1954), 29.

2. Jonathan D. Sarna, *American Judaism: A History* (New Haven: Yale University Press, 2004), 64.

3. Ibid., 65.

4. Kurt F. Stone, *The Jews of Capitol Hill: A Compendium of Jewish Congressional Members* (Lanham, Md.: Scarecrow Press, 2011), 8.

5. Details of Jewish life in Charleston available in Charles Reznikoff, *The Jews of Charleston: A History of an American Jewish Community* (Philadelphia: Jewish Publication Society of America, 1950), and Barnet A. Elzas, *The Jews of South Carolina: From the Earliest Times to the Present Day* (Spartanburg, S.C.: The Reprint Company, 1972).

6. Pierce Butler, *Judah P. Benjamin* (Philadelphia: G. W. Jacobs, 1907), 32.

7. Butler, *Judah P. Benjamin*, 26.

8. Jennie Holton Fant, *The Travelers' Charleston: Accounts of Charleston and Lowcountry South Carolina, 1660–1861* (Columbia: University of South Carolina Press, 2016).

9. Details of black life in Charleston in Walter J. Fraser Jr., *Charleston! Charleston!* (Columbia: University of South Carolina Press, 1989), and Maureen Dee McInnis, *The Politics of Taste in Antebellum Charleston* (Chapel Hill: University of North Carolina Press, 2005).

10. Douglas R. Egerton, *He Shall Go Out Free: The Lives of Denmark Vesey* (Lanham, Md.: Rowman & Littlefield, 2004), 183.

11. Ibid., 191.

12. Sarna, *American Judaism*, 43.

13. Ibid., 54, 43.

14. Elzas, *The Jews of South Carolina*, 160–61.

15. Sarna, *American Judaism*, 84–87.

16. Details of Benjamin's life at Yale in Meade, *Judah P. Benjamin*.

17. Ibid., 25–30.

18. Lawley Mss., Center for Jewish History, New York.

Chapter 2. New Orleans

1. Thomas Ruys Smith, *Southern Queen: New Orleans in the 19th Century* (London: Continuum, 2011), 72–73.

2. Ibid., 64.

3. Frederick Law Olmsted, *A Journey to the Sea-board Slave States: With Remarks on Their Economy* (New York: Dix and Edwards, 1856), 583.

4. See Shirley Elizabeth Thompson, *Exiles at Home: The Struggle to Become American in Creole New Orleans* (Cambridge: Harvard University Press, 2009).

5. In Meade, *Judah P. Benjamin*, plate facing p. 57.

6. Bertram Wallace Korn, *The Early Jews of New Orleans* (Waltham, Mass.: The American Jewish Historical Society, 1969).

7. Cited in Andrew Delbanco, *The War Before the War: Fugitive Slaves and the Struggle for America's Soul from the Revolution to the Civil War* (New York: Penguin, 2019), 90

8. J. S. Whitaker, *Sketches of Life and Character from Louisiana: The Portraits Selected Principally from the Bench and Bar* (New Orleans: Ferguson & Crosby, 1847), 27.

9. Varina Davis, letter in Lawley Mss.

10. Evans, *Judah P. Benjamin*, 91.

11. William Howard Russell, *My Diary North and South* (Philadelphia: Temple University Press, 1988), 167.

12. Bertram Korn, *Jews and Negro Slavery in the Old South, 1789–1865* (Philadelphia: Maurice Jacobs, 1961), 15–25.

13. Saul S. Friedman, *Jews and the American Slave Trade* (New Brunswick, N.J., Transactions, 1998), 166.

14. See Richard Follett, *Sugar Masters: Planters and Slaves in Louisiana's Cane World, 1820–1860* (Baton Rouge: Louisiana State University Press, 2005).

15. Butler, *Judah P. Benjamin*, 50.

16. *De Bow's Review*, January 1848.

17. Walter Johnson, *Soul by Soul: Life Inside the Antebellum Slave Market* (Cambridge: Harvard University Press, 2009), 23.

18. Follett, *Sugar Masters*, 64.

19. Frederick Bancroft, *Slave-Trading in the Old South* (Baltimore: J. H. Furst, 1931), 312.

20. *Proceedings and Debates of the Convention of Louisiana* (New Orleans, 1845), February 14, 1845.

21. *Proceedings and Debates*, May 8, 1845.

22. Meade, *Judah P. Benjamin*, 73–74.

23. G. G. Vest, *The American Israelite*, October 15, 1903 (originally printed in *The Saturday Evening Post*).

24. "Blake Pontchartrain on the Boston Club," *Behind NOLA's Closed Doors*, February 28, 2011 (http://bostoncluboncanal.blogspot.com/2011/02/blake-pontchartrain-on-boston-club.html).

25. Judah Benjamin, letter to Samuel L. M. Barlow, in Judah P. Benjamin Collection, Historic New Orleans Archive, Mss. 33.1.

26. Butler, *Judah P. Benjamin*, 99–100.

Chapter 3. Washington

1. See Daniel Walker Howe, *The Political Culture of the American Whigs* (Chicago: University of Chicago Press, 1979).

2. Meade, *Judah P. Benjamin*, 96.

3. Korn, *Eventful Years and Experiences*, 65.

4. Butler, *Judah P. Benjamin*, 147.

5. *Congressional Globe*, July 18, 1854.

6. Joanne B. Freeman, *The Field of Blood: Violence in Congress and the Road to Civil War* (New York: Farrar, Straus & Giroux, 2018), 236.

7. Meade, *Judah P. Benjamin*, 104.

8. Evans, *Judah P. Benjamin*, 97.

9. Butler, *Judah P. Benjamin*, 175.

10. Varina Davis, letter in Francis Lawley Mss.

11. *Congressional Globe*, May 2, 1856.

12. Meade, *Judah P. Benjamin*, 156.

13. Jonathan D. Sarna and Benjamin Shapell, *Lincoln and the Jews: A History* (New York: St. Martin's, 2015), 66–69).

14. Robert F. Durden, *The Gray and the Black: The Confederate*

Debate on Emancipation (Baton Rouge: Louisiana State University Press, 1972), 18.

15. John Stuart Mill, *The Subjection of Women* (Cambridge: MIT Press, 1974), 13, 11.

16. Judah P. Benjamin and Peter Hargous Correspondence, 1857–60, in American Jewish Historical Society Archives.

17. Meade, *Judah P. Benjamin*, 121.

18. Ibid., 122.

19. Ibid., 124.

20. William Seale, *To Live on Lafayette Square: Society and Politics in the President's Neighborhood* (Washington, D.C.: The White House Historical Association, 2019), 89.

21. Virginia Clay-Clopton, *A Belle of the Fifties: Memoirs of Mrs. Clay of Alabama, Covering Social and Political Life in Washington and the South, 1853–1866* (New York: Doubleday, Page, 1904), 52–54.

22. For debate over *Dred Scott*, see Alan Nevins, *Ordeal of the Union*, vol 2 (New York: Collier, 1992).

23. *Congressional Globe*, March 11, 1858.

24. Butler, *Judah P. Benjamin*, 97–99.

25. Varina Davis, letter in Lawley Mss.

26. Burton J. Hendricks, *Statesmen of the Lost Cause: Jefferson Davis and His Cabinet* (Boston: Little, Brown, 1939).

27. Evans, *Judah P. Benjamin*, 65.

28. Ibid., 69–70.

29. Hendricks, *Statesmen of the Lost Cause*, 41.

30. Evans, *Judah P. Benjamin*, 98–99.

31. *Congressional Globe*, May 22, 1860.

32. Meade, *Judah P. Benjamin*, 127–34.

33. Evans, *Judah P. Benjamin*, 108.

34. *Congressional Globe*, December 31, 1860.

35. Evans, *Judah P. Benjamin*, 110.

36. Christian F. Eckloff, *Memoirs of a Senate Page (1855–1859)* (New York: Broadway Publishing, 1909), 56.

37. G. G. Vest, *The American Israelite*, October 15, 1903 (originally printed in *The Saturday Evening Post*).

38. Phillips's story is told in Robert N. Rosen, *The Jewish Con-*

federates (Columbia: University of South Carolina Press, 2000), 284–96, and in Samuel Proctor and Louis Schmier, "Eugenia Levy Phillips: The Civil War Experiences of a Southern Jewish Woman," in *Jews and the Civil War*, ed. Jonathan D. Sarna and Adam Mendelsohn (New York: NYU Press, 2010).

39. *Congressional Globe*, February 4, 1861.

Chapter 4. Richmond

1. William Howard Russell, *My Diary North and South* (Philadelphia: Temple University Press, 1988), 125–27.

2. Butler, *Judah Benjamin*, 160.

3. Evans, *Judah Benjamin*, 119.

4. Ibid., 116.

5. Ibid., 120.

6. Ibid., 121.

7. Varina Davis letter in Lawley Mss.

8. Varina Davis, *Jefferson Davis, Ex-President of the Confederate States: A Memoir* (New York: Belford, 1890), 163.

9. Meade, *Judah P. Benjamin*, 187.

10. Varina Davis letter.

11. Evans, *Judah P. Benjamin*, 153.

12. Benjamin to Johnston, September 27, 1861, in *The War of the Rebellion: A Compilation of the Official Records of the Union and Confederate Armies* (Washington: Government Printing Office, 1880–1901), vol. 4, 430.

13. Benjamin to Johnston, September 29, 1861, in ibid., vol. 5, 885.

14. Davis to Benjamin, November 10, 1861, in ibid., vol. 5, 955.

15. Wood to Benjamin, November 20, 1861, in ibid., vol. 4, 401.

16. Meade, *Judah P. Benjamin*, 209.

17. Benjamin to Brig. Gen. William H. Carroll, December 10, 1861, in *The War of the Rebellion*, vol. 7, 754.

18. Evans, *Judah P. Benjamin*, 132–33.

19. Ernest B. Furgurson, *Ashes of Glory: Richmond at War* (New York: Knopf, 1996), 56–57.

20. Thomas Cooper De Leon, *Belles, Beaux, and Brains of the '60s* (New York: G. W. Dillingham, 1909), 93.

21. Varina Davis letter.

22. Benjamin to McCullouch, November 30, 1861, in *The War of the Rebellion*, vol. 8, 700.

23. Evans, *Judah P. Benjamin*, 123–25.

24. Meade, *Judah P. Benjamin*, 215–18.

25. John B. Jones, *A Rebel War Clerk's Diary* (New York: Sagamore, 1958), October 31, 1861, December 4, 1861, December 10, 1861.

26. Evans, *Judah P. Benjamin*, 145.

27. C. Vann Woodward, ed., *Mary Chesnut's Civil War* (New Haven: Yale University Press, 1981).

28. Henry S. Foote, *Casket of Reminiscences* (Washington, D.C.: Chronicle, 1874), 151.

29. Evans, *Judah P. Benjamin*, 200–202.

30. Stephen Vincent Benét, *John Brown's Body* (New York: Doubleday, Doran, 1928), verses 68–69.

31. Evans, *Judah P. Benjamin*, 147.

32. Letter to Francis Lawley.

33. Sallie Brock Putnam, *Richmond During the War Years: Four Years of Personal Observation* (Lincoln: University of Nebraska Press, 1996), 99.

34. Meade, *Judah P. Benjamin*, 180.

35. See Emory M. Thomas, *The Confederate State of Richmond* (Austin: University of Texas Press, 1971) and Ernest B. Furgurson, *Ashes of Glory: Richmond at War* (New York: Knopf, 1996).

36. Foote, *Casket of Reminiscences*, 209.

37. Varina Davis, *A Memoir*, 526.

38. Evans, *Judah P. Benjamin*, 224–25.

39. Jones, *War Diary*, May 7, 1863.

40. Mrs. Burton Harrison, *Recollections Grave and Gay* (New York: Scribner's Sons, 1911), 160.

41. Varina Davis, *A Memoir*, 207.

42. David Brown, *Palmerston: A Biography* (New Haven: Yale University Press, 2010), 451.

43. Evans, *Judah P. Benjamin*, 195.

44. Jasper Ridley, *Lord Palmerston* (London: Anchor, 1970), 554.

45. Mason to Benjamin, July 30, 1862, in *Official Records of the Union and Confederate Navies in the War of the Rebellion*, Series II, vol. 3 (Harrisburg, Pa.: National Historical Society, 1987), 490.

46. Mason to Robert Hunter, March 26, 1862, in ibid., 372.

47. Benjamin to Slidell, April 12, 1862, in ibid., 387.

48. Slidell to Benjamin, July 25, 1862, in ibid., 481.

49. Benjamin to Slidell, July 9, 1862, in ibid., 461.

50. Gary Philip Zola, *We Called Him Father Abraham: Lincoln and American Jewry, a Documentary History* (Carbondale: Southern Illinois University Press, 2014), 59.

51. Sarna and Shapell, *Lincoln and the Jews*, 142; Daniel Brook, "The Forgotten Confederate Jew," *Tablet*, July 17, 2012 (www.tabletmag.com/jewish-arts-and-culture/books/106227/the-forgotten-confederate-jew).

52. Benjamin to Mason, May 20, 1863, in *Official Records*, 774.

53. Benjamin to Mason, December 11, 1862, in ibid., 619.

54. Frederick Bancroft, *The Life of William H. Seward*, vol. 2 (New York: Harper and Brothers, 1909), 312.

55. Slidell to Benjamin, July 30, 1862, in *Official Records*, 490.

56. Eric Foner, *The Fiery Trial: Abraham Lincoln and American Slavery* (New York: W. W. Norton, 2010), 245.

57. Bancroft, *Life of Seward*, 341–42.

58. Hotze to Benjamin, September 14, 1863, in *Official Records*, 923.

59. Benjamin to Hotze, January 9, 1864, in ibid., 994.

60. Bancroft, *Life of Seward*, 349.

61. Robert N. Rosen, *The Jewish Confederates* (Columbia: University of South Carolina Press, 2000), 156.

62. Benjamin to Slidell, July 12, 1864, *Official Records*, 1072.

63. William A. Tidwell, *April '65: Confederate Covert Action in the American Civil War* (Kent, Ohio: Kent State University Press, 2014), 131.

64. Jane Singer, *The Confederate Dirty War: Arsons, Bombings,*

Assassinations, and Plots for Chemical and Germ Attacks on the Union (Jefferson, N.C.: McFarland, 2005), 26–43.

65. Evans, *Judah P. Benjamin*, 264.

66. Singer, *The Confederate Dirty War*, 51–62.

67. Thompson letter to Benjamin, December 4, 1864, in Microfilm Reel 6, Confederate States of America Records.

68. Washington letter to Lawley, Lawley Mss.

69. Benjamin to Capston, July 3, 1863, in *Official Records*, 828.

70. Benjamin to Hotze, September 15, 1864, in *Official Records*, 1206.

71. Benjamin to Slidell, December 27, 1864, in ibid., 1253.

72. Robert F. Durden, *The Gray and the Black: The Confederate Debate on Emancipation* (Baton Rouge: LSU Press, 1972), 102–5.

73. Ibid., 183.

74. Ibid., 182–83.

75. Evans, *Judah P. Benjamin*, 275.

76. Butler, *Judah P. Benjamin*, 351.

77. Meade, *Judah P. Benjamin*, 307–8.

78. Evans, *Judah P. Benjamin*, 282–85.

79. Furgurson, *Ashes of Glory*, 320.

80. Evans, *Judah P. Benjamin*, 294.

81. Ibid., 295.

Chapter 5. Flight

1. Furgurson, *Ashes of Glory*, 321.

2. Varina Davis letter to Lawley.

3. Evans, *Judah P. Benjamin*, 299.

4. Ibid., 301–2.

5. Mrs. Burton Harrison, *Recollections Grave and Gay* (New York: C. Scribner's Sons, 1912), 223.

6. Evans, *Judah P. Benjamin*, 358.

7. William A. Tidwell with James O. Hall and David Winfred Gaddy, *Come Retribution: The Confederate Secret Service and the Assassination of Lincoln* (Jackson: University Press of Mississippi, 1988), 19–22, 291, 409.

8. Ibid., 418.

9. Evans, *Judah P. Benjamin*, 340.

10. Singer, *The Confederate Dirty War*, 121, 123.

11. Ibid., 137.

12. Evans, *Judah P. Benjamin*, 308–9.

13. Ibid., 311–12.

14. Ibid.

15. Quoted in Butler, *Judah P. Benjamin*, 363.

16. Rosen, *The Jewish Confederates*, 322.

17. Evans, *Judah P. Benjamin*, 318.

18. Ibid., 319.

19. Ibid., 321.

Chapter 6. London

1. Butler, *Judah P. Benjamin*, 228.

2. Ibid., 371.

3. Letter to Bradford, February 21, 1866. Francis Lawley Mss. in Pierce Butler Collection.

4. Evans, *Judah P. Benjamin*, 329–30.

5. Ibid., 382.

6. Ibid., 386–87.

7. Evans, *Judah P. Benjamin*, 345.

8. Butler, *Judah P. Benjamin*, 389.

9. "Did One Man Write The First Great English Dictionary All By Himself?" *Dictionary.com* (https://www.dictionary.com/e/johnson/).

10. Judah P. Benjamin, *Benjamin's Treatise on the Law of Sale of Personal Property: With Reference to the American Decisions and the French Code of Civil Law* (Indianapolis: Bowen-Merrill, 1899).

11. Meade, *Judah P. Benjamin*, 335.

12. Butler, *Judah P. Benjamin*, 390.

13. Evans, *Judah P. Benjamin*, 349.

14. Butler, *Judah P. Benjamin*, 372.

15. Foote, *Casket of Reminiscences*, 285.

16. Meade, *Judah P. Benjamin*, 342–43.

17. Ibid., 341–42.

18. Evans, *Judah P. Benjamin*, 368.

19. Meade, *Judah P. Benjamin*, 338.

20. Evans, *Judah P. Benjamin*, 378.

21. Meade, *Judah P. Benjamin*, 372.

22. Evans, *Judah P. Benjamin*, 381.

23. Butler, *Judah P. Benjamin*, 405–6.

24. Ibid., 407.

25. Ibid., 408.

26. Ibid., 430–31.

27. Meade, *Judah P. Benjamin*, 366–67.

28. Butler, *Judah P. Benjamin*, 410.

29. Letter to Francis Lawley, September 12, 1882, in Pierce Butler Collection.

30. Butler, *Judah P. Benjamin*, 413.

31. Evans, *Judah P. Benjamin*, 397–98.

32. Benjamin to Lawley, April 23, 1884, in Lawley Mss.

ACKNOWLEDGMENTS

I HAD A LOT of help both researching and writing this book. As for the first, I owe thanks to the archivists who taught me local history and helped me locate documents, including Leon Miller at the Louisiana Research Collection in New Orleans, Dale Rosengarten at the Jewish Heritage Collection of the College of Charleston, Nic Butler at the Charleston Public Library and Karen Brickman Emmons at the Historic Charleston Foundation. I received wise editorial counsel from, as always, my son Alex; Leonard Groopman; Claire Potter and other members of my writers group: David Greenberg, James Goodman, Michael Massing, James Ledbettter, Matthew Connelly, and Dahlia Lithwick. My agent, Andrew Wylie, took care of everything, as he always does. I benefited greatly from the copy-editing labor of the gracious and very patient Phillip King. Above all, I would like to thank Ileene Smith, my friend and editor and general editor of the Yale Jewish Lives series, who brought me the idea, nurtured me through the process, and very gently prodded me to make changes that she surely knew I needed to make.

INDEX

Abendanone, Hannah, 11
abolitionism, 2, 16, 30; Benjamin's
    view of, 44–45, 51–52, 58, 60; in
    British Commonwealth, 104; in
    Europe, 113–14; among Jews, 59.
    See also slavery, slaves
Adams, Charles Francis, 105, 111–12
Adams, John Quincy, 1, 30, 31, 58
American and Foreign Anti-Slavery
    Society, 59
American Party (Know-Nothings),
    50, 51
Amistad case (1841), 1, 30
Antietam, Battle of (1862), 111
Aristotle, 60
Articles of Confederation, 74
Atlanta, 119, 123
Atzerodt, John, 134

Bacon, Francis, 22
Ball's Bluff, Battle of (1861), 84–85
Bancroft, Frederick, 43

Barlow, Samuel, 48, 74
Battle of Antietam (1862), 111
Battle of Ball's Bluff (1861), 84–85
Battle of Buena Vista (1847), 69
Battle of Five Forks (1865), 125
Battle of Fredericksburg (1862), 111
Battle of Gettysburg (1863), 109
Battle of Seven Days (1862), 100, 109
Bayard, James, 68, 71
Bayard, Thomas, 54, 142, 153, 157,
    160
Beauregard, P. G. T., 81, 82, 83, 92–93,
    130
Beecher, Henry Ward, 59
Belden, R. C., 12
Bellechasse (plantation), 2, 35–36,
    38–40
Belle of the Fifties (Clay-Clopton), 65
Benét, Stephen Vincent, 3, 96–97
Benjamin, Alexander, 142
Benjamin, Hatty (sister), 103, 142
Benjamin, Joseph (brother), 103, 157

Benjamin, Judah P.: anti-Semitism and, 95–98; as barrister, 147–50, 154–56, 159; birth of, 9; in Charleston, 10–19, 23; as Confederate attorney general, 2, 79, 80, 82; as Confederate secretary of state, 2, 101–27; as Confederate secretary of war, 2, 83, 85–98; Confederate victory foreseen by, 108–9, 110–11, 115; cotton deal sought by, 106–8; Davis cultivated by, 83–84; Davis's feud with, 67–68, 70–71; Davis's resignation urged by, 137; death of, 162; Douglas denounced by, 71; education of, 12–13; espionage and sabotage plots and, 114–19; finances of, 47–48, 156, 157; Francophilia of, 34; French abolitionism viewed by, 113–14; as gambler and card player, 22, 48, 54, 101; homosexuality imputed to, 4, 37, 38, 95, 97, 110; industriousness of, 2, 6, 84, 91, 148, 159; Kansas-Nebraska Act opposed by, 56–57; legal career of, 1–2, 7, 29–33, 46, 47, 61, 73, 147–50, 154–56, 159; legal writings of, 7, 29, 149–50, 156; Lincoln kidnapping plot and, 133, 134–35; Lincoln's assassination and, 131–32, 136, 139; in London, 144–59, 160; marriage of, 28–29, 35–38, 144; *McCargo* case argued by, 1–2, 30–31, 44, 59; in New Orleans, 25–49; in Paris, 144, 159–63; physical appearance of, 32–33, 55; as planter, 39–41, 47–48; post-surrender flight of, 138–43, 151; rail links backed by, 46–47, 61–64; realism of, 80–81; resilience of, 7, 163; as rhetorician, 1–2, 19, 51–54, 75–76, 79–80, 91, 123–25, 155; secretiveness of, 4; secularism of, 3, 5, 13, 19, 33–34; slave conscription sought by, 121–25, 154; as slaveowner, 2, 3,

36, 41–43, 58; slavery defended by, 2–6, 32, 44–45, 56–58, 67, 72; sociability of, 3, 20–21; as state legislator, 43–44, 49; Supreme Court seat declined by, 61; surrender rejected by, 130–31; unctuousness of, 89–90; Union peace terms rebuffed by, 109–10; as U.S. senator, 2, 5, 49–50, 64–65, 67–68, 70–72, 74–75; urbanity of, 54; voice of, 33; Washington residences of, 64–66; at Yale, 19–22
Benjamin, Lionel (nephew), 103
Benjamin, Natalie (St. Martin; wife), 35, 38, 90, 144, 145, 157; at Benjamin's death, 162–63; marriage of, 5, 28–29; in Paris, 5, 36–37, 39, 54, 61, 65, 158, 159–60; rumors surrounding, 37, 46, 64, 65
Benjamin, Ninette (daughter), 5, 36–37, 39, 54, 61, 144, 157–58, 160
Benjamin, Penina (sister), 103, 139–45, 149, 159
Benjamin, Philip (father), 9–13, 18, 19
Benjamin, Rebecca (Mendes; mother), 9, 12, 13, 19
Benjamin (Levy), Rebecca (sister), 9, 38, 48, 103, 150, 158
Benjamin on Sales, 149–50, 156
Beth Elohim (Charleston, S.C.), 11, 17–19
Bevis Marks Synagogue (London), 17
Booth, John Wilkes, 131–36
Bousignac, Henri de, 157–58
Bradford, E. A., 145
Breckinridge, John C., 72, 152
Brooks, Preston, 53
Brown, Joseph E., 86
Bryant, William Cullen, 66
Buchanan, James, 61–62, 63
Buena Vista, Battle of (1847), 69
Bull Run, First Battle of (1861), 82, 84, 92
Burnside, Ambrose, 98
Butler, Benjamin, 88, 110–11
Butler, Pierce, 6, 12, 39–40, 42, 58, 96

Calhoun, John C., 20, 56, 69
California, 46, 50
Capston, J. J., 119, 135
Cardozo, Isaac, 18–19
Cardozo, Jacob, 11
Cass, Lewis, 62
Castillero, Andres, 73
Charleston, S.C.: economic troubles in, 23; free blacks and hired-out slaves in, 13, 14–15; Jewish settlement of, 10–12; slavery's centrality to, 14, 16–17; synagogue in, 11, 17–19
Charleston Mercury, 53
Chesnut, James, 90
Chesnut, Mary, 90, 95
City Gazette, 11, 16
Clark, Henry T., 86
Clay, Clement C., 65, 113
Clay, Henry, 43, 50, 56, 64, 122
Clay-Clopton, Virginia, 65
Cleburne, Patrick, 120
Cobb, Howell, 95, 121
Cobb, Thomas R. R., 95
Cobden, Richard, 113
Come Retribution (Tidwell, Hall, and Gaddy), 133, 135
Comonfort, Ignacio, 63
A Confederate Spy (Conrad), 133
Conover, Samuel, 132
Conrad, F. B., 30
Conrad, Thomas, 133
Constitutional Convention, 74
Copperheads, 116
cotton, 23, 25, 81, 106
Creole case, 1–2, 30–31, 44, 59

Dahlgren, Ulric, 133–34
Daily Telegraph, 145
Davis, A. W. G., 86–87
Davis, Jefferson, 4, 55, 78, 81, 87, 96, 102, 108, 122, 132; arrest of, 139, 142, 151; Benjamin's feud with, 67–68, 70–71; Benjamin's indispensability to, 2, 83–84, 99, 103; generals' obstreperousness toward, 92–94; Lincoln

kidnapping plot and, 133, 136; in London, 154; marriages of, 68–69; military aspirations of, 80, 82, 83; postwar charges against, 152–53; Richmond evacuations led by, 99–100, 125–27; slavery proposal by, 120–21; surrender and resignation rejected by, 129–30, 137–38; zealotry of, 69, 79
Davis, Joseph, 69
Davis, Sarah Knox (Taylor), 68–69
Davis, Varina (Howell), 68, 70, 80, 82, 90, 99, 101, 103, 138, 152; Benjamin's financial support for, 151; Benjamin viewed by, 3, 33, 55, 75, 84, 91, 162; as Lost Cause adherent, 154; marriage of, 69
Day, Jeremiah, 21
De Bow's Review, 40
Decatur, Stephen, 64
Decatur House, 64–65
de Leon, Edwin, 113, 115
De Leon, Thomas Cooper, 89–90
Delta (newspaper), 49, 51
Democratic party, 44, 49, 50, 57, 59, 66, 71, 116–17
Deslonde, Mathilde, 65
Disraeli, Benjamin, 5, 146
Douglas, Stephen A., 55–56, 71–72, 76
Douglass, Frederick, 112
Dred Scott v. Sandford (1857), 66–67, 71
Dumas, Alexandre, 60
Dunham, Charles, 132
Dwight, Timothy, 20

Early, Jubal, 82
Eckloff, Christian F., 76
Eggleston, George Cary, 89
Emancipation Proclamation (1862), 112
Enquirer (Richmond newspaper), 98
Evans, Eli, 83, 132
Examiner (Richmond newspaper), 96

Fearon, Henry, 25
Field, Stephen, 47
Fillmore, Millard, 60–61

First Battle of Bull Run (1861), 82, 84, 92
Five Forks, Battle of (1865), 125
Florida, 44
Follett, Richard, 41
Foote, Henry S., 95–96, 101, 153
Forsyth, Lewis, 62
Fredericksburg, Battle of (1862), 111
free-soilers, 56, 64, 71
Fugitive Slave Act (1850), 50, 52, 61

Garay, José de, 61
Gautier, Théophile, 60
Gettysburg, Battle of (1863), 109
Giddings, Joshua Reed, 58
Gladstone, William, 104, 146
Grant, Ulysses, 118, 122, 125, 126, 127, 130, 137
Grimké, Angelina, 16
Grimké, Sarah, 16

Haiti, 15, 57, 113–14
Hale, John P., 54
Hamilton, Alexander, 2
Hannibal (servant), 14
Harby, Isaac, 11, 12, 16, 18, 23
Hargous, Peter A., 46, 61–63
Harney, Thomas, 134–35, 136
Harrison, Burton, 131
Harrison, Constance Cary, 102
Haussmann, Georges Eugène, baron, 159
Headley, James, 118
Hebrew Orphan Society, 12
Hotze, Henry, 108, 113–14, 115, 119
Howell (Davis), Varina. See Davis, Varina (Howell)
Hunter, Robert, 99, 106
Hyams, Henry, 46
Hyde de Neuville, Anne-Marguerite-Henriette Rouillé de Marigny, baronne, 64

Irving, William, 126

Jackson, Andrew, 88
Jackson, Thomas "Stonewall," 82, 83, 94

James, Henry (attorney general), 7, 161
James, William Milbourne, 155
Jefferson, Thomas, 32, 81
John Brown's Body (Benét), 3, 96–97
Johnson, Andrew, 88, 142
Johnson, Reverdy, 47, 73
Johnson, Samuel, 149
Johnston, Albert Sidney, 85–86
Johnston, Joseph, 82, 83, 86, 92, 126, 137; Benjamin rebuked by, 94–95; surrender urged by, 130
Jones, John B., 95, 102
Journey to the Sea-Board Slave States (Olmsted), 26
Juárez, Benito, 63, 106

Kansas-Nebraska Act (1854), 51, 54, 55–56, 67, 76
Kansas Territory, 71
Kenner, Duncan, 90, 122, 125
Kentucky Resolution (1798), 74
Know-Nothings (American Party), 50, 51
Korn, Bertram, 29, 36

Latrobe, Benjamin, 64
Latrobe, Charles, 24, 25
Laurens, Henry, 13
Lawley, Francis, 4, 22, 119, 162
Lee, Robert E., 83, 125, 129; Davis contrasted with, 68; at Drewry's Bluff, 99–100; at Gettysburg, 109; postwar charges against, 152; Richmond evacuation urged by, 126; slave conscription and, 120, 123; surrender of, 130, 137
Leovy, Henry J., 138, 139
Letcher, John, 94
Levy, Jacob, 9, 12, 14
Levy, Leah (niece), 38, 48, 103
Levy, Moses, 11
Levy, Rebecca (Benjamin), 9, 38, 48, 103, 150, 158
Levy (Yulee), David, 11, 55, 65–66
Liberal party, 103, 112
Lincoln, Abraham, 68, 73, 77, 122; assassination of, 131–36, 139, 152;

Douglas vs., 71–72; kidnapping plot aimed at, 133–35; peace overtures by, 109, 112; reelection of, 115, 116, 119; volunteers called up by, 81
Lopez, Moses, 12, 19
Louisiana, 77
Louis-Philippe, king of the French, 65

Mallory, Stephen, 128
Mann, Dudley, 108
Mansfield, William Murray, Earl of, 31
Margaret (maid), 14
Marshall, Charles, 98
Martin, Samuel, 150
Mason, George, 105
Mason, James, 75, 104–5, 106, 108, 111, 113
McCargo, Thomas, 30, 31
McCargo v. Merchants Insurance (1845), 1–2, 30–31, 44, 59
McClellan, George B., 100, 109
McCullouch, Ben, 91–92
McDowell, Irvin, 82
McRae, Colin, 155
Meade, Robert Douthat, 6, 57–58, 59, 63
Mendes (Benjamin), Rebecca (mother), 9, 12, 13, 19
The Merchant of Venice (Shakespeare), 2, 3, 31
Mercier, Henri, 109
Meredith, Minerva, 101
Merrimack (ironclad), 99
Mexican War, 69, 70
Michigan (steamer), 117
Mill, John Stuart, 60
Missouri Compromise, 55–56, 67
Monitor (ironclad), 99
Morse, Jedediah, 25
Murphy, Dennis, 76

Napoleon III, emperor of the French, 105–6, 107, 111, 112
Nashville Convention (1850), 70
Nefuzoth Yehudah (Touro Synagogue), 33–34

Negro Seaman Act (Louisiana, 1822), 52
New Mexico, 50
New Orleans: economic boom in, 25, 29–30, 45–46; ethnic diversity in, 24, 35; Jewish slaveowners in, 36; racial hierarchy in, 27–28, 31–32; sexual mores in, 25–26, 37–38; slave market in, 27, 41, 43; synagogue in, 33–34; Union seizure of, 88, 103
Newport, R.I., 10
New York City, 10, 118
New York Times, 152, 156, 160
North Carolina, 74, 81
Northup, Solomon, 41
nullification, 74

"Ode on the Death of Lord Wellington" (Tennyson), 131, 163
Olmsted, Frederick Law, 26
Overend, Gurney & Company, 145

Packwood, Theodore, 39, 40, 48
Palmerston, Henry John Temple, Viscount, 104–5, 111, 113, 125, 156
Panic of 1819, 23
Paul, Alfred, 126
Phillips, Aaron, 10
Phillips, Eugenia Levy, 77
Phillips, Philip, 11, 76–77
Phineas Finn (Trollope), 156
Pierce, Franklin, 55, 61, 70
The Plot Against America (Roth), 4, 136
Polk, James Knox, 69
Pollock, Charles Edward, 147, 148
popular sovereignty, 55, 56, 66, 71
Porcher, Charles, 122
Putnam, Sallie Brock, 99

Randolph, John, 54
Raphall, Morris Jacob, 59
Reconstruction, 158
Reformed Society of Israelites, 18
Renan, Ernest, 60
Republican party, 59, 66
Revue des Deux Mondes, 60, 113

Rhode Island, 74
Richmond, 88–90, 99–101, 122–27, 129
Richmond Whig (newspaper), 118
Rillieux, Norbert, 41
Roanoke Island, N.C., 97–99
Roth, Philip, 4
Russell, John Russell, Earl, 104, 105, 156
Russell, William Howard, 34–35, 78–79
Rutledge, John, 13

St. Martin, Auguste, 28
St. Martin, Jules, 36, 90–91, 128–29, 136, 138, 158
St. Martin, Natalie. *See* Benjamin, Natalie (St. Martin)
Sarna, Jonathan D., 10, 17
Savannah, Ga., 10, 120, 123
Schiff, Jacob, 26
secession, 74, 77
Seddon, James Alexander, 102, 133
Seixas, Abraham, 16
Selborne, Roundell Palmer, Earl of, 161
Sentinel (Richmond newspaper), 120
Seven Days, Battle of (1862), 100, 109
Seward, William H., 104, 105, 112
Shearith Israel (New York City), 17
Sheridan, Philip, 129
Sherman, William Tecumseh, 119–20, 137
Shiff, Hart, 26
Simons, Moses, 20
Sketches of America (Fearon), 25
slavery, slaves: agrarianism perpetuated by, 85; Benjamin's defense of, 2–6, 32, 44–45, 56–58, 67, 72; in Charleston, 14, 16–17; Davis's proposal for, 120–21; European views of, 112–14; "hired-out," 13, 15; Jewish complicity in, 16, 36, 59; legal arguments against, 30–31; Mill's view of, 60; nation riven by, 50–57, 70, 71, 73–74, 120; revolts and mutinies by, 15, 30, 57, 113–14; in Richmond, 89, 100; on

sugar plantations, 39, 41–43. *See also* abolitionism
Slidell, John, 65, 120; as Benjamin's patron, 29, 44, 46, 49, 61, 144; as Confederate commissioner to France, 104–9, 111, 112, 115, 116; Union seizure of, 104–5
Slidell, Tom, 29–30, 44, 46
Sloo, A. G., 61–62
Snyder, William H., 135
Somerset v. Stewart (1772), 31, 56, 66, 67
Sons of Liberty, 116–17, 119
South Carolina, 16–17, 74
Southern Patriot, 11
Stephens, Alexander, 90
Stidger, Felix Grundy, 117
Stoneman, George, 131
Stringer, Greenbury, 28
Stroyer, Jacob, 41
Stuart, A. H. H., 115–16
Stuart, Jeb, 82, 102
The Subjection of Women (Mill), 60
sugar, 39–43
Sumner, Charles, 52–53, 66, 113
Surratt, John, 132, 134–35

Taylor (Davis), Sarah Knox, 68–69
Taylor, Zachary, 46, 68
Tennyson, Alfred Tennyson, Baron, 131
Texas, 44
Thompson, Jacob, 116–19, 131, 132
tobacco, 88–89, 129
Tory party, 104, 113, 146, 156
Touro, Judah, 26, 33, 38
Touro Synagogue (Nefuzoth Yehudah), 33–34
Tredegar Iron Works, 85, 100
Tresca, Frederick, 140
Trollope, Anthony, 156
Twelve Years a Slave (Northup), 41

U.S. v. The Amistad (1841), 1, 30

Van Buren, Martin, 64
Van Lew, Elizabeth, 127
Vattel, Emer de, 74

Vesey, Denmark, 15, 57
Vest, George Graham, 47, 76
Virginia, 81
Virginia Resolution (1798), 74

Wade, Benjamin, 5, 54
Walker, LeRoy, 79, 80–81, 83
Washington, I. Q., 119
Webster, Daniel, 34
Weill, Abram, 136
Weld, Theodore Dwight, 58
Whig party (Great Britain), 103–4
Whig party (U.S.), 43–44, 49, 50–51, 57, 61
Whitaker, J. S., 32–33

Wigfall, Louis, 153, 154, 155, 157
Winder, John H., 101, 114
Wirz, Henry, 152
Wise, Henry, 98
Wise, Isaac Mayer, 34
Wise, Jennings, 98–99
Witt, Joseph G., 157
Wood, John Taylor, 139
Wood, W. B., 87–88

Yale University, 19–22
yellow fever, 13, 25
Yulee (Levy), David, 11, 55, 65–66

Zacharie, Issachar, 109

PUBLISHED TITLES INCLUDE:

Rabbi Akiva: Sage of the Talmud, by Barry W. Holtz
Ben-Gurion: Father of Modern Israel, by Anita Shapira
Bernard Berenson: A Life in the Picture Trade, by Rachel Cohen
Irving Berlin: New York Genius, by James Kaplan
Sarah: The Life of Sarah Bernhardt, by Robert Gottlieb
Leonard Bernstein: An American Musician, by Allen Shawn
Hayim Nahman Bialik: Poet of Hebrew, by Avner Holtzman
Léon Blum: Prime Minister, Socialist, Zionist, by Pierre Birnbaum
Louis D. Brandeis: American Prophet, by Jeffrey Rosen
Martin Buber: A Life of Faith and Dissent, by Paul Mendes-Flohr
David: The Divided Heart, by David Wolpe
Moshe Dayan: Israel's Controversial Hero, by Mordechai Bar-On
Disraeli: The Novel Politician, by David Cesarani
Einstein: His Space and Times, by Steven Gimbel
Becoming Freud: The Making of a Psychoanalyst, by Adam Phillips
Emma Goldman: Revolution as a Way of Life, by Vivian Gornick
Hank Greenberg: The Hero Who Didn't Want to Be One,
    by Mark Kurlansky
Peggy Guggenheim: The Shock of the Modern, by Francine Prose
Ben Hecht: Fighting Words, Moving Pictures, by Adina Hoffman
Heinrich Heine: Writing the Revolution, by George Prochnik
Lillian Hellman: An Imperious Life, by Dorothy Gallagher
Theodor Herzl: The Charismatic Leader, by Derek Penslar
Houdini: The Elusive American, by Adam Begley

Jabotinsky: A Life, by Hillel Halkin

Jacob: Unexpected Patriarch, by Yair Zakovitch

Franz Kafka: The Poet of Shame and Guilt, by Saul Friedländer

Rav Kook: Mystic in a Time of Revolution, by Yehudah Mirsky

Stanley Kubrick: American Filmmaker, by David Mikics

Stan Lee: A Life in Comics, by Liel Leibovitz

Primo Levi: The Matter of a Life, by Berel Lang

Groucho Marx: The Comedy of Existence, by Lee Siegel

Karl Marx: Philosophy and Revolution, by Shlomo Avineri

Menasseh ben Israel: Rabbi of Amsterdam, by Steven Nadler

Moses Mendelssohn: Sage of Modernity, by Shmuel Feiner

Harvey Milk: His Lives and Death, by Lillian Faderman

Moses: A Human Life, by Avivah Gottlieb Zornberg

Proust: The Search, by Benjamin Taylor

Yitzhak Rabin: Soldier, Leader, Statesman, by Itamar Rabinovich

Walther Rathenau: Weimar's Fallen Statesman, by Shulamit Volkov

Jerome Robbins: A Life in Dance, by Wendy Lesser

Julius Rosenwald: Repairing the World, by Hasia R. Diner

Mark Rothko: Toward the Light in the Chapel,
    by Annie Cohen-Solal

Gershom Scholem: Master of the Kabbalah, by David Biale

Bugsy Siegel: The Dark Side of the American Dream,
    by Michael Shnayerson

Solomon: The Lure of Wisdom, by Steven Weitzman

Steven Spielberg: A Life in Films, by Molly Haskell

Alfred Stieglitz: Taking Pictures, Making Painters, by Phyllis Rose

Barbra Streisand: Redefining Beauty, Femininity, and Power,
    by Neal Gabler

Leon Trotsky: A Revolutionary's Life, by Joshua Rubenstein

Warner Bros: The Making of an American Movie Studio,
    by David Thomson

FORTHCOMING TITLES INCLUDE:

Franz Boas, by Noga Arikha

Mel Brooks, by Jeremy Dauber

Alfred Dreyfus, by Maurice Samuels

Elijah, by Daniel Matt

Anne Frank, by Ruth Franklin

Betty Friedan, by Rachel Shteir

George Gershwin, by Gary Giddins

Allen Ginsberg, by Ed Hirsch

Ruth Bader Ginsburg, by Dorothy Samuels

Herod, by Martin Goodman

Abraham Joshua Heschel, by Julian Zelizer

Jesus, by Jack Miles

Josephus, by Daniel Boyarin

Louis Kahn, by Gini Alhadeff

Maimonides, by Alberto Manguel

Louis B. Mayer and Irving Thalberg, by Kenneth Turan

Golda Meir, by Deborah E. Lipstadt

Arthur Miller, by John Lahr

Robert Oppenheimer, by David Rieff

Ayn Rand, by Alexandra Popoff

Man Ray, by Arthur Lubow

Sidney Reilly, by Benny Morris

Hyman Rickover, by Marc Wortman

Philip Roth, by Steven J. Zipperstein

Edmond de Rothschild, by James McAuley

Ruth, by Ilana Pardes

Jonas Salk, by David Margolick

Rebbe Schneerson, by Ezra Glinter

Baruch Spinoza, by Ian Buruma

Henrietta Szold, by Francine Klagsbrun
Elie Wiesel, by Joseph Berger
Billy Wilder, by Noah Isenberg
Ludwig Wittgenstein, by Anthony Gottlieb